A Guided Journal for the Deaf and Hard of Hearing

Becoming
HEARING EMPOWERED

Katherine S. Rybak

SHINE
PRESS

Cover Design: Kaitlin Walsh of Lyon Road Art

For permission requests and ordering information, email the author at:
katherine@hearingoutloud.net

ISBN: 979-8-9909367-2-0

REVISED EDITION

For more information about the author, to book her for your next event,
media interview, or bulk orders, please contact her at:
katherine@hearingoutloud.net

SHINE PRESS serves entrepreneurs and business owners with a dedicated focus on high quality at affordable prices with an excellent author experience.

Make Your Book *SHINE.*
ShinePressBooks.com

words of praise

I was born with a progressive severe to profound hearing loss, had two sisters with a similar loss, and my best friend had a loss that was nearly a copy of mine. My parents were dynamic, had resources, and did all they could to ensure we grew up to become well-adapted adults. Despite all these enormous advantages, I wish that I had been a beneficiary of Katherine Rybak's book.

Hearing and hearing loss are incredibly complex subjects, far more complex than the popular view that one either hears or does not hear. Her work enables us to learn the basics about hearing loss, but more importantly, she understands the intrapersonal and emotional struggles of hearing loss and enables us to learn diverse ways to manage those struggles. The emotional difficulties many of us with hearing loss experience are rooted in how we do or don't successfully communicate and relate with others from a confident core understanding of self.

Katherine's work is ground-breaking in that she goes beyond the fundamentals and enables us to learn how to interact with others and self-advocate in a way that is positive and promotes both respect and self-respect. Some of us learn how to do this even without this book, but the path is often inefficient and can be painful. It can take years of trial and error.

—*Jack Spear, Ph.D.* in Psychology, President of the Madison,
WI Chapter of the Hearing Loss Association of America

*This book is dedicated to Carol, my wife,
who has been my biggest cheerleader and supporter.
Her love and encouragement empowered me
to get this book from my heart to the page.*

contents

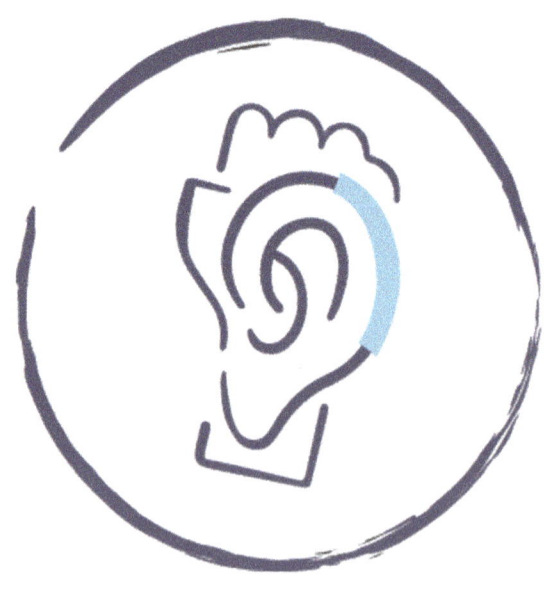

1 | preparation

Hello and welcome. I am Katherine from *Hearing Out Loud,* and I will be your guide throughout the pages of the *Becoming Hearing Empowered: A Guided Journal for the Deaf and Hard of Hearing.*

Since I was a child, I have experienced progressive hearing loss that has fluctuated due to multiple surgeries. I've slowly learned how to interact with the world differently with each change in my hearing levels.

I remember getting my first hearing aid as an elementary student and feeling a little embarrassed talking about it. I wanted to call it something other than a "hearing aid," and my friend and I, using the first letters in "hearing aid," decided to call it my "haha." It only came in silly putty beige, and the purpose of this color was to make it "less noticeable" in my ear. And now I ask myself, "Why? Why do people choose glasses in fun, bright colors? My hearing aid looked like a wad of gum. Where was that feeling of stigma and shame coming from?" It was, and still is, so embedded in our society, and even children feel a sense of shame about their hearing loss.

As an adult, I became a Teacher for the d/Deaf and Hard of Hearing because I wanted to break down the stigma of hearing loss, build a sense of pride in our unique identity and encourage children with hearing loss to become self-advocates.

I've expanded this work to adults as I meet more and more people struggling with internalized stigma about their hearing loss. Internalized stigma is when a person with hearing loss (consciously or unconsciously) takes in the negative messages and stereotypes about hearing loss and begins to believe them. On average, it takes 7 years for a person with hearing loss to seek help. Imagine going 7 years unable to read the text on your phone because you fear glasses will make you look old. Adults who develop hearing loss have not had the benefit of a Teacher of the d/Deaf and Hard of Hearing to guide them through the experience, empower them with confidence, teach them about available technology, encourage them to be a self-advocate, and provide a list of useful accommodations. These adults are on their own to fumble through learning how to live with a condition that cuts them off from family, friends, and community because hearing loss directly impacts their ability to communicate effectively and connect with the people they love.

But it isn't easy. Many of us feel as if we don't belong. We are surrounded by the hearing culture, where communication is primarily auditory verbal, and the sense of hearing is required to hear and comprehend the conversation. In general, people in the hearing world make the assumption that all of us can hear and understand spoken language with ease. Verbal exchanges are fast-paced, filled with figurative language and slang, and often intolerant of communication breakdowns. We have learned that when we miss something, we may be judged as inattentive, rude, or slow. Our need for clarification slows the pace of the interchange, people lose interest, and we feel left behind. It only takes a few times of being told, "never mind," before we start to think maybe it's better just to bluff or disengage from the conversation entirely.

Many of us don't know other people who have hearing loss. Those of you who developed hearing loss in your adult lives, or are late-deafened, may experience isolation and don't know where to turn. As a teacher, I help my students understand the science of hearing, teach them how to advocate for a variety of accommodations, and encourage them to develop a positive self-identity. As adults, there's usually not someone readily available who can help us navigate this experience.

This is why I have created this guided journal, a place where you can give yourself the time and space you deserve to deconstruct your internalized stigma on hearing loss, discover empowerment with a growth mindset, apply mindfulness during communication, redraw your boundaries, reframe your identity, reclaim your confidence and rediscover the joy of connecting with the people you love.

A Word About Words

There are so many words that are used to describe difficulty in hearing, including deaf, hearing loss, hearing impaired, hard of hearing, late-deaf, Deaf, hearing disability, late deafened—I'm sure there are more. And there are some significant emotions that go along with some of these terms. For you, some labels may feel disrespectful or inappropriate for a number of reasons. We will discuss this more in Chapter 5: Identity & Self Love, but for now, please know that I will be using many of these terms interchangeably in an effort to expose you to them, allow you to try them on for yourself, and to give you the opportunity to develop your own thoughts about the language we use to describe our hearing experience. However, as an umbrella term, and for the sake of simplicity, I will most often use the term "hearing loss" when referring to all of these.

Becoming Hearing Empowered

The term "hearing impaired" has often been used to describe people with hearing loss; however, it has been widely rejected in the hearing loss community. "Impaired" is defined as "weakened or damaged." While this may be true in terms of the physical process of hearing, it implies that the person is somehow weak or damaged. With the time you spend working through the pages of this book, you can transform your experience of "impairment" and discover a sense of true empowerment.

Overview

The guided journal is designed to be completed at your own pace. It consists of a daily log, spaces to record your reflections, activities to explore concepts learned in the chapters, and blank pages to use in your own creative way. The daily log can help you plan your experience in a way that works best for you and help you stay on track.

The time it takes to complete the journal activities really depends on you because you can take as little or as much time as you need to write and express yourself with words or images.

This experience is completely self-paced, but if you like, you can create a schedule for yourself. You may want to spend 1 week on each of the 8 chapters, finishing the journal in 2 months' time. Or, you can create a weekend retreat for yourself, where you plan to complete the journal over a few days. However you choose to budget your time, committing yourself to a plan created ahead of time will ensure your completion of all the activities of each chapter.

Book Clubs

You may also enjoy using this journal as part of a book club with other people who have hearing loss. If you think this could be valuable, and you've found a couple peers to work with, I've included some resources on the website you are free to use. If you are a member of a hearing loss organization, such as the Hearing Loss Association of America (HLAA) or the Association of Late Deafened Adults (ALDA), the book can provide many ideas for workshops or small group meetings.

 Check out hearingoutloud.net for guides and suggestions.

This is Not Therapy

It is important to remember that this guided journal can not take the place of seeing a qualified therapist, psychologist, or psychiatrist if you are struggling with mental health challenges such as depression, anxiety, and other diagnoses. I have lived with depression and anxiety since childhood, and I understand the depths of these illnesses. The sole intent of this journal is to provide a structure of information, guidance, and exercises that will build your positive sense of self as it relates to hearing loss. If you experience intense feelings of sadness, fearfulness, anxiety, or depression, please contact a professional.

Preparing for the Journal Activities

Before we dive into new learning and activities, you need to be sure you have everything you need to be fully present and prepared to make the most out of each day you spend in the journal.

Your Audiogram

In chapter three, you will be learning about the science of hearing and how to read an audiogram. To prepare for this, if you've had your hearing tested, contact your clinic to get a printed copy of your most recent audiogram. If you haven't had your hearing tested or do not have access to an audiogram, a sample audiogram will be available to you in chapter three to use as practice.

Journal

At the back of the book, you will find multiple "Daily Log" pages. For each block of time, you spend working in the journal, use a Daily Log page to document your progress, plan your next session, and end your work session with a positive affirmation.

The information written in each chapter will introduce the concepts and provide instructions on how to approach the journal activities. To get the most out of your time and energy with each journal activity, be sure to complete them after you've read through the preceding information.

If you find you need more space to write or draw when completing a journal activity, flip to the very back of your journal and use the numbered blank pages there. In the original journal prompt, jot down the page number of the blank page(s) you used so you can easily find where your thoughts are continued at the back of the book.

Supplies

Gather your writing and drawing materials. Find your favorite pens or pencils and keep them with this book. YYou may also want to gather some other art supplies, such as markers (PaperMate Flair and Sharpie S-Note are good options), colored pencils, oil pastels, gel pens, colored paper, fabric, glue stick, or any other supplies that come to mind for you. Many of the activities include the opportunity to express your thoughts and feelings in whatever way you choose, including writing, making a list, drawing, and using color. Gather your supplies and keep them in one location, such as a box or tote bag, so they are easily accessible for each section.

Space

Find a quiet setting where you can spend time alone without distractions. You might want to arrange for childcare or find a location where you can be assured of no interruptions. Some exercises will require you to write, so wherever you are, plan to have a hard surface and a comfortable place to sit. Some things to keep in mind may be sunscreen if you'll be outdoors or a sign for the door asking not to be disturbed. Whatever you need to do to create a space where you can give yourself the time and attention you need to work through each section of the journal.

Schedule

Consider the time needed to complete each section, including the time to read and complete each activity. On average, you can plan about 10 minutes per activity; however, some will take less, and some will take more. Grab your calendar and create a schedule that works for you. You will also want to consider the time you need to prepare yourself emotionally at the start of each section and the time you may need to transition back to your day-to-day life. If you need to take more than one sitting to complete any of the activities in a chapter, please stop whenever you need, complete your daily log, including choosing a positive affirmation, and make a commitment to return where you left off next time.

PREPARATION CHECKLIST
JOURNAL ACTIVITY

[] Obtain a copy of your audiogram (if you've had a hearing test) from your audiologist or clinic

[] Gather writing and art supplies

[] Create a schedule

[] Prepare your space

[] Complete your First Thoughts and Feelings Journal entry

[] Complete the Daily Log

FIRST THOUGHTS & FEELINGS
JOURNAL ACTIVITY

You've decided to work through this book as a way to learn more about living with hearing loss and how to develop feelings of empowerment. It is an opportunity to consider the ways your hearing loss impacts you emotionally, how you identify yourself, improving communication with the important people in your life, and implementing self-care strategies. What are your thoughts and feelings right now about this book and how you hope it will improve your life?

_____

_____

_____

_____

_____

_____

_____

_____

_____

_____

_____

_____

_____

_____

_____

DAILY LOG

For each day working through the activities in this book,
use a Daily Log page at the back of your journal
to document your progress, plan your next session,
and end your session with a positive affirmation.
Many sample affirmations are available in the back of the journal.

Every time you see this icon,
the session is complete and it is your cue to complete your daily log.

2 | mindset

Section One

Before we begin this chapter, let's take a look at some common thoughts you might have as a person with hearing loss.

MINDSET STATEMENTS
JOURNAL ACTIVITY

Read through each statement on the next two pages and circle the thoughts you have or have had in the past. I encourage you to resist judging yourself and know that it's natural to have a wide range of thoughts and feelings that change from day to day. Got some thoughts you don't see here? Add your own! This is just an exercise to find out more about yourself. Be honest with yourself. You deserve the truth.

I can get a job in the field I am passionate about because I can self-advocate for accommodations that will make me successful.

My hearing loss is ruining my life.

My hearing technology is amazing and I like it when people notice it!

I'm not deaf enough. I'm not hearing enough. I don't fit in anywhere.

My hearing loss enriches my life--I've met people and had experiences I wouldn't have had if it weren't for my hearing loss.

I can't establish the kind of relationship I want with _____ because of my hearing disability.

My partner/friend/relative/coworker cares about our relationship and appreciates learning strategies and being reminded of strategies that help me hear and understand them.

I don't have a friend group because of my hearing disability.

I have a set of strategies that make parties, even loud parties, something I can enjoy.

My partner/friend/relative/coworker never remembers the strategies that help me understand them--they just don't care enough.

My hearing loss is unique--but I know I'm not the only one.

I appreciate it when people ask questions about my hearing disability.

I can't work in the professional field I am passionate about because of my hearing impairment.

Despite my hearing impairment, I can develop a deep and meaningful relationship with _____.

Life would be so much better if I had normal hearing.

I hate parties.

My partner wants to understand how my hearing disability affects me, but doesn't understand yet.

I hope _____ doesn't notice my hearing aid/cochlear implant.

I have a community of people that understand my experience.

My friendships are better because I talk about my hearing loss and how my friends can support me.

I hate it when people talk about my hearing loss.

I won't find a partner who truly understands me and how to communicate with me.

I embrace and strive to find new ways to improve my life with hearing loss.

Other:

_____

_____

_____

_____

_____

_____

_____

_____

Introduction

A key foundation to your success in this whole process is your mindset. Everything you do and feel and believe can be profoundly influenced by your mindset. It can reframe your beliefs about what you are capable of, and open new opportunities to discover empowerment. Researchers have discovered the power of mindset, and its principles are being applied in schools, businesses, relationships and parenting. How do we think about our talents, our abilities, our disabilities, our skills? Can the way we think about these things be changed? How do these thoughts influence our success in our jobs, our friendships, our families and our favorite pastimes?

In this chapter, we are going to learn what mindset is, why it is important, the difference between fixed and growth mindsets, and how to nurture your own growth mindset.

Chapter 2 Goals:

- I can state in my own words what mindset means.
- I can give three reasons why mindset is important.
- I can describe the difference between fixed and growth mindsets.
- I know how to nurture my own growth mindset.

What is Mindset?

Mindset is defined as the established set of attitudes held by someone. Mindset is the attitude and the words you use to talk to yourself when you've encountered a frustrating situation. A mindset is developed by thinking and reflecting on your experiences; changing your thinking patterns and the way you reflect on your experiences changes your mindset and the way you view the world. And because you have created your mindset by thinking, you can also change your mindset with new thinking.

Let's think about a possible scenario to illustrate how mindset works. Maybe you find yourself at a friend's house, ready to watch a movie together, and they start the movie without closed captions enabled. You wait a few minutes to see if your friend realizes you need the captions on, and when they continue to watch the movie and munch popcorn, you feel invisible and angry. Maybe tonight is the last straw in a frustrating week filled with little moments like this. You've experienced many times when you were excluded from a conversation because the background music was too loud, or when you missed something important at work because a co-worker made a verbal announcement instead of sending an email, and when you felt out of touch because the hilarious TikTok video everyone was talking about isn't captioned. Just living the daily life of a hard or hearing or d/Deaf person.

Your thoughts and feelings are fueled and validated by your current mindset. What happens next is determined by your mindset. Maybe you grab the remote with annoyance to turn the captions on, continuing to watch the movie but inwardly obsess on the many times your friend has failed to acknowledge your hearing disability. Or, perhaps you give up entirely, snap at your friend that you're leaving, and tell yourself that you really didn't like them that much anyway. Maybe you grab the remote, pause the movie, and tell your friend you are struggling and hurt. Your outlook determines which thoughts and feelings are the most obvious to you in the moment, and plays a huge role in which thoughts and feelings you act on. I can see myself reacting in all of these ways, but there is only one of these responses that I know will feed my sense of empowerment and support my positive self-esteem. But that option, pausing the movie and talking about your feelings, may feel like the hardest choice for you right now. Maybe you are telling yourself, "What's the point? Something like this will just happen again tomorrow. Hard of hearing = left out. There's nothing I can do about it."

This is where mindset can change your life.

Mindset can profoundly affect the way you live your life, and in our case, the way you live your life with hearing loss. Your mindset can determine how you successfully connect with others in your social life, your work and your relationship with your partner(s).

If you have spent much of your lifetime feeling defeated before you even began, your world may be filled with frustration, anger and disappointment. You may feel as though your circumstances are what prevent you from living the life you want. Maybe you feel that your hearing loss, your childhood, your difficult relationships all hold you back and are the reason you see closed door after closed door. Perhaps you think you are limited, and your only hope for success is if you can just prove yourself, if someone would just give you a break, and if you can successfully hide your past failures.

You can reframe your life with a different mindset. You can find opportunity after opportunity to grow and become who you've always wanted to be, because of and in spite of your hearing loss, your childhood, your difficult relationships. You can persevere in the face of adversity. You can expand and develop and change and adapt. Discover your inner strength, build your self-esteem, and develop empowering advocacy skills that will improve your relationships and move you forward on a new path in your life. This is 100% possible for you, for all of us. This is the power of mindset.

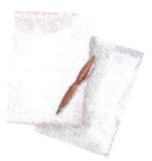

Section Two

In this section, we are going to learn about two mindsets: the fixed mindset and the growth mindset.

Fixed Mindset

A fixed mindset is the belief that who you are, your abilities, and your role in life are already predetermined. You are stuck with the cards you've been dealt. You have been set on a certain path because of where you were born, who your parents are, what you have experienced, your degree of hearing loss, your IQ, and more. It feels like changing that path would be difficult, if not impossible! You find yourself constantly trying to prove that you are good enough, smart enough, capable enough, hearing enough, deaf enough. You have accepted that because of your hearing loss, you will just miss out on many things in life that others seem to take for granted. You will miss out on friendships, parties, relationships, jobs, jokes, conversations, and connections. There's not much you can do about it.

A fixed mindset influences your relationships, as well. With a fixed mindset, you may look at many aspects of your relationship with your significant other, parent, child, friend, or sibling as established. The way in which you talk to each other, react to each other, and relate to each other is basically how it's always been and how it will always be. You may look at that person as having a certain degree of emotional intelligence, a personality that won't change much over time. This may feel like good news, or not so great news, depending on how compatible you are with these characteristics. There may be pieces of your relationship that don't feel quite right, but you don't believe you can do much to change them.

People with fixed mindsets are more likely to give up in the face of challenging circumstances because they believe they are stuck. The fixed mindset is an internal dialogue focused on judgment and avoidance of making mistakes.

Growth Mindset

A growth mindset is the belief that who you are, your abilities, and your role in life can all be cultivated and changed. Through hard work, strategies and support from others, you can change the trajectory of your life! Yes, you have been dealt a certain set of circumstances, but they do not have to determine your degree of success, your ability to reach your goals, or the quality of your relationships. Your place of birth, your family, your hearing loss, your past experiences are all just the starting point on your path to happiness and empowerment because you can grow and change. Your true potential is not predetermined--it is unknown. It is impossible to predict what you can accomplish with passion, work, support and new learning.

A growth mindset can profoundly influence your relationships. With a growth mindset, you may look at aspects of your relationship as fluid and moldable, as well as the skills of those that you love. The ways you talk, react, and relate to each other is adaptable and how it is now is not necessarily how it will always be. Your partner may not yet have the skills to be empathetic with your hearing loss; the person they are will grow and change over time. There may be pieces of your relationship that don't feel quite right, but with a growth mindset you believe you can learn how to be better, together.

People with growth mindsets are more likely to persevere in the face of setbacks. Instead of throwing in the towel, adults with a growth mindset view it as an opportunity to learn and grow. The growth mindset is an internal dialogue focused on learning and growing and constructive action.

The key here is to stop trying to prove yourself, stop hiding your hearing loss, stop nodding your head when you don't understand, stop telling yourself you can't because you can't hear.

Embrace this opportunity to learn and grow. Find out what you can accomplish when you believe that you can develop new skills and strategies. Give yourself the time and space to become empowered and become your own best advocate.

WHAT MINDSET DO I HAVE?
JOURNAL ACTIVITY

Find two markers, crayons or highlighters. Choose one color for fixed mindset and the other color for growth mindset. Color them in here:

Fixed Mindset	**Growth Mindset**

Now, go back to the statements you circled earlier in this module. Reread them and, based on what you've learned about mindset, decide if they represent a fixed mindset or a growth mindset. Color just the ones you circled with your two colors. Remember, no one else needs to see this, so there is no judgment here. Just be honest with yourself.

Reflection: What have you discovered? Have most of your thoughts fallen into a fixed mindset or a growth mindset? This is a non-judgmental opportunity to simply observe the thoughts you've had about your hearing loss. Be proud of the work you are doing today and know you are taking steps toward becoming empowered.

_____

_____

_____

_____

_____

_____

_____

_____

_____

Section Three

In this section, you will learn the benefits of changing your mindset from a fixed mindset to a growth mindset.

Changing Your Mindset

Growth mindset gives you another way to be. With a growth mindset, you have another way to confront challenges, approach difficult obstacles, focus your efforts, interpret criticism, and be inspired by the success of others.

A fixed mindset pressures you to avoid challenges, such as participating in a group discussion that would expose the fact that you can't hear as well as others in the group, something you've been trying to hide. A growth mindset embraces this challenge and uses it as a platform to educate others about hearing loss, or views it as an opportunity to practice self-advocacy by using assistive listening devices or real-time captioning to improve your access to the discussion.

A fixed mindset urges you not to bother learning sign language or not even to continue working through the chapters of this book. Why expend the energy learning something new when it won't make any difference and would just be a waste of time? A growth mindset applauds your efforts of learning new ways to communicate and practicing self-advocacy skills. The fruits of this labor can only lead to empowerment and increased self-esteem.

It's important to note that changing your mindset isn't like flipping a switch. Chances are, even if you move on to embrace a growth mindset, your inner voice will sometimes make judgments and urge you to hide your hearing aids, nod your head when you don't understand, or storm out of your friend's house when they don't turn on the captions. Growth mindset sheds new light on these moments and gives you another opportunity to grow, give yourself some grace, and step into your power.

Need some extra help shifting your fixed mindset to a growth mindset? Try these out.

Embrace the Journey.

Recognize that there is value in the work you are doing. It is not about achieving a certificate of completion, it is about learning, growing and evolving. Your participation in this guided journal is an experience that will allow you to reflect on your life, discover how you think about your hearing and make changes that leave you feeling empowered.

Embrace the Power of "Yet."

Add this word to your inner dialogue frequently. Instead of saying you can't do something, say you haven't learned how to do it yet. "With my hearing loss, I just can't function at a dinner party." "I haven't figured out how to enjoy myself at a dinner party yet." Open yourself to other ways to enjoy attending a dinner party if that is what you want to do. Maybe you want to try using a remote microphone with your friend so the two of you can have a conversation while others talk amongst themselves. Maybe you try a captioning app on your phone to understand your friend better. Maybe you request to sit at the middle of the table instead of the head of the table so you can see and hear most of the people you're dining with.

Pay Attention to How You Talk to Yourself.

Remind yourself to be non-judgemental. Encourage yourself with positive affirmations. Be patient with yourself. Take on challenges as a way to grow and discover what you can be when you allow yourself to think differently. Allow yourself to make mistakes and use them as opportunities to learn.

REFRAMING
JOURNAL ACTIVITY

Take a look back at the journal activity "Mindset Statements" that you completed at the beginning of this chapter. If many of the thoughts you circled are worded in a fixed mindset, can you imagine reframing them in a growth mindset? Your thoughts, your beliefs and the words you use to talk to yourself are powerful! They can shape your future. Even though you might not believe them right now, try rewriting two of your fixed mindset thoughts so they now come from a growth mindset.

_____
_____
_____
_____
_____
_____
_____
_____
_____
_____
_____
_____
_____
_____
_____
_____

I encourage you to reread what you have just written. Try reading it aloud to yourself. I invite you to consider posting this on your bathroom mirror or as your phone's lock screen, and use it as a daily affirmation. Can you imagine yourself actually believing it? What happens when you believe the growth mindset thoughts to be absolutely true?

This is the end of chapter two. Return to the *Reframing* page in your journal over the next few days if you have more than two fixed mindset statements circled and rewrite all of them using a growth mindset. Use your Daily Log to assign a few future days you will do this. Continue to reflect on how these reframed thoughts can improve your quality of life with a hearing disability.

If you'd like to learn more about mindset, check out the book *Mindset: The New Psychology of Success* by Carol Dweck.

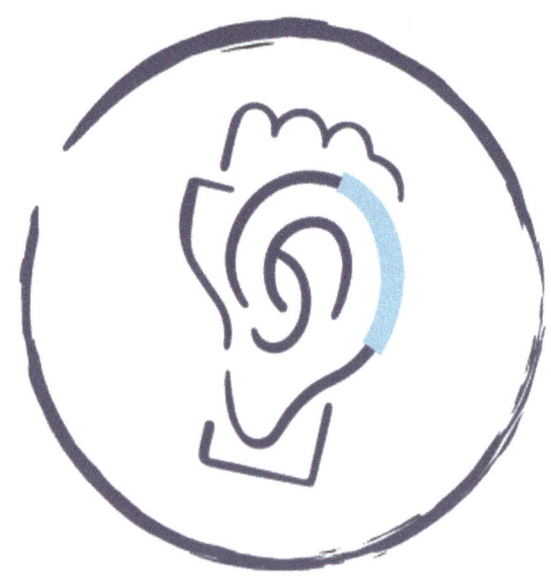

BECOMING HEARING EMPOWERED

3 | hearing loss 101

Section One

In this section, we'll go over the goals for this chapter. And you're going to learn the basics of ear anatomy.

Chapter 3 Goals:

- I understand the value of learning about ear anatomy and audiograms.
- I can locate, label and state the function of all parts of the outer, middle, inner ear.
- I can sequence the process of hearing.
- I can describe the three types of hearing loss and locate the parts of the ear that are affected on a diagram.
- I can describe the difference between an air conduction and bone conduction hearing test, and the purpose of masking.
- I can describe the information provided on an audiogram.
- I can describe the limitations of a hearing test.
- I can describe my hearing in more than one way using my current audiogram.

DESCRIBE YOUR HEARING LOSS
JOURNAL ACTIVITY

Describe your hearing loss, and try to think of the words and terms you use most often. You may have more than one way you do this, depending on who you are talking to. Try to record all the ways and words you use to describe your hearing loss.

_____

_____

_____

_____

_____

_____

_____

_____

_____

_____

_____

_____

_____

_____

_____

_____

_____

_____

Introduction

In chapter three, Hearing Loss 101, you will learn the basic science of hearing loss. Understanding how the ear works, how we process sound and what part(s) of the ear aren't working properly is important information for you to know. Learning how to read your audiogram can broaden your understanding of your hearing loss and how you function in different listening situations. We will also go over how to describe your hearing loss accurately, which is important for others to understand that your hearing experience is more complex than "everything is quieter."

This information is absolutely essential if you are to make informed decisions about future treatments, technology and accommodations you may use in your life. It provides you with a strong foundation to understand and track your hearing ability, and help you determine what works best for you. Understanding your hearing loss gives you the confidence to make difficult decisions and tackle new challenging situations.

As you work through this chapter, use the labeled ear anatomy diagram, audiogram key, and sample audiogram which are included here for your reference.

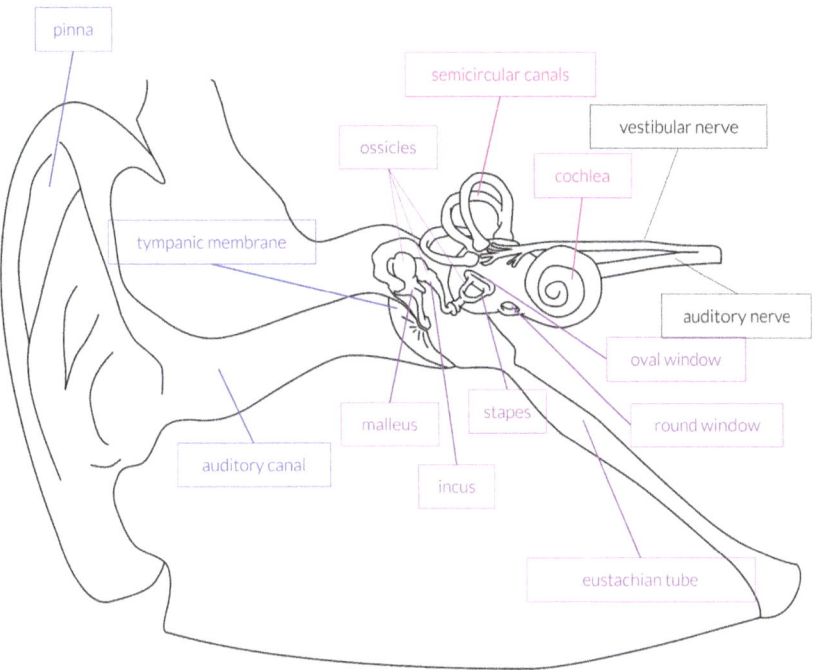

Sample Audiogram

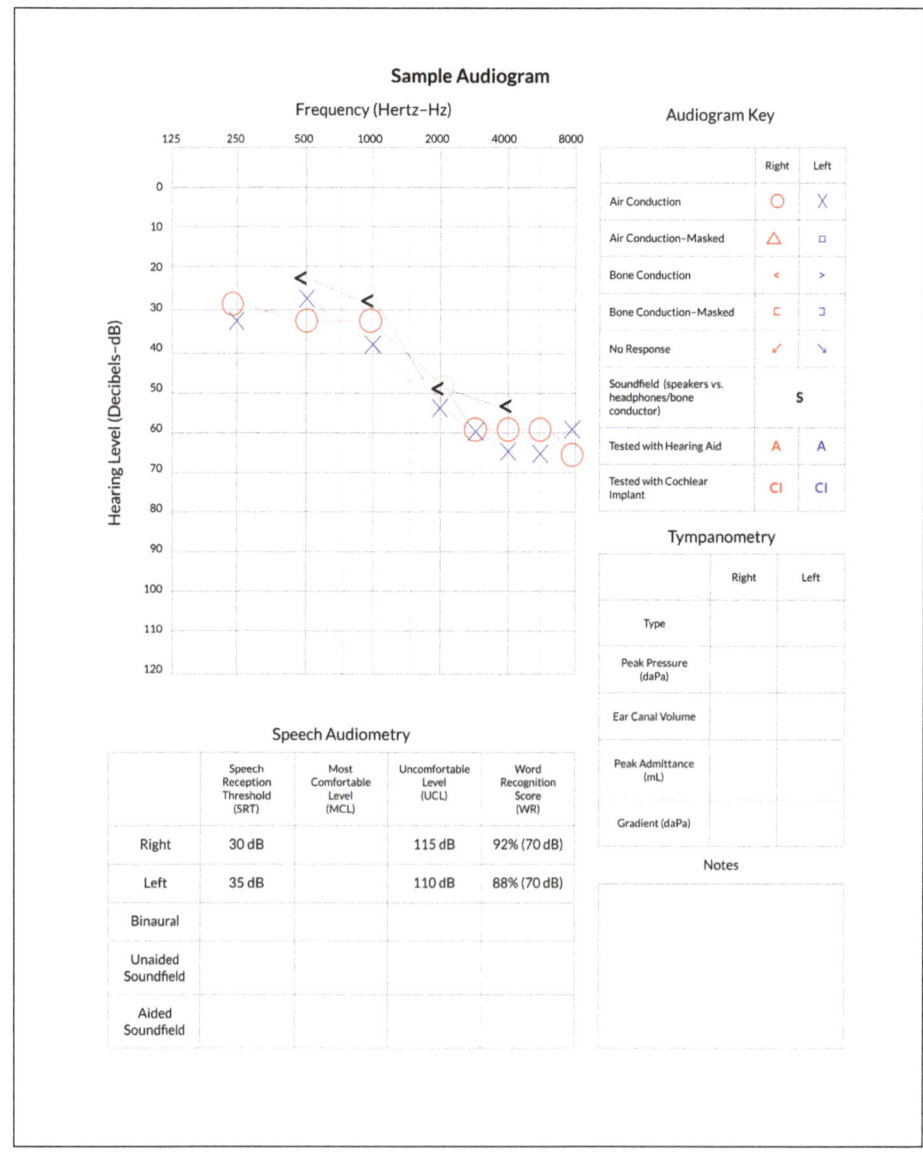

Frequency (Hertz–Hz)

Audiogram Key

	Right	Left
Air Conduction	◯	✕
Air Conduction–Masked	△	☐
Bone Conduction	‹	›
Bone Conduction–Masked	⊏	⊐
No Response	↙	↘
Soundfield (speakers vs. headphones/bone conductor)	S	
Tested with Hearing Aid	A	A
Tested with Cochlear Implant	CI	CI

Tympanometry

	Right	Left
Type		
Peak Pressure (daPa)		
Ear Canal Volume		
Peak Admittance (mL)		
Gradient (daPa)		

Speech Audiometry

	Speech Reception Threshold (SRT)	Most Comfortable Level (MCL)	Uncomfortable Level (UCL)	Word Recognition Score (WR)
Right	30 dB		115 dB	92% (70 dB)
Left	35 dB		110 dB	88% (70 dB)
Binaural				
Unaided Soundfield				
Aided Soundfield				

Notes

Ear Anatomy

Ear anatomy is often split into three main areas: the outer ear, the middle ear, and the inner ear.

The outer ear includes the pinna, the auditory canal, and tympanic membrane (which is also called the eardrum).

The middle ear includes tiny bones called the ossicles: the malleus, the incus, and the stapes. These bones are also frequently called the hammer, the anvil and the stirrup, because of their shapes. The oval window and the round window, along with the eustachian tube, are also considered part of the middle ear. The middle ear should be a dry, air-filled space.

The inner ear includes the cochlea and semicircular canals. The auditory nerve connects to the cochlea and transmits electrical sound signals to the brain. The vestibular nerve connects to the semicircular canals and transmits signals to the brain that regulate balance. This is why vertigo, or dizziness, can sometimes occur with certain types of hearing loss. Both the cochlea and the semicircular canals are fluid-filled with tiny receptors that create electrical signals.

 If you are a visual learner, check out hearingoutloud.net for links to some helpful videos.

DIAGRAM OF THE EAR
JOURNAL ACTIVITY

Label the diagram with the names of parts you just learned. If you like, use your art supplies to color and decorate the image as well. You can refer to the labeled diagram located earlier in the chapter if you get stuck.

Labels:

outer ear

middle ear

inner ear

pinna

ear canal

tympanic membrane (eardrum)

ossicles (malleus, incus, stapes)

eustachian tube

cochlea

oval window

round window

auditory nerve

semicircular canals

vestibular nerve

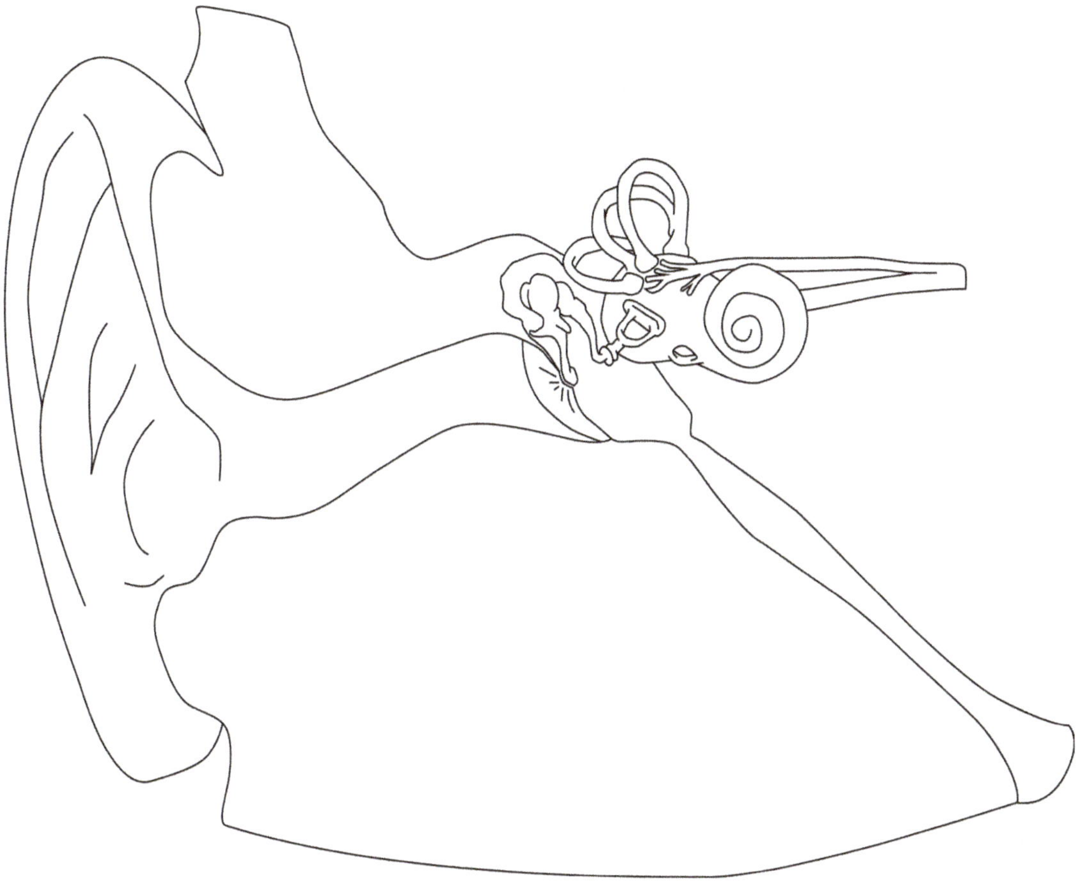

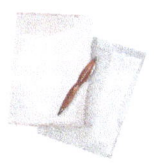

Section Two

In this section, you will learn about the complex process of hearing and the three types of hearing loss. Then you will complete a journal activity.

The Process of Hearing

The actual process of hearing is incredibly complex. We receive sound in two ways; the first process of hearing is called air conduction, and the second is through bone conduction.

Understanding how air conduction hearing and bone conduction hearing work will be important when we talk about your audiogram in upcoming lessons. Please note, if you're a visual learner, you may want to check out YouTube for a couple videos illustrating the process of hearing.

In air conduction, what begins as a sound pressure wave funneled in by the outer ear becomes mechanical energy as it moves through the bones in the middle ear, becomes hydraulic energy inside the cochlea of the inner ear, which finally becomes electrical energy as it is sent through the auditory nerve to the brain. Let's look at this process a little closer.

The pinna acts like a funnel, capturing the sound waves around you and sending them through the auditory canal. When the sound waves reach the tympanic membrane, it begins to vibrate like a drum. The vibration moves the ossicles in the middle ear; first the malleus, then the incus, and finally the stapes. The stapes pushes inside the oval window, creating tiny waves in the liquid of the cochlea. The round window bulges outward in response to the pressure. Inside the cochlea, tiny hair cells, or stereocilia, move in response to the waves, similar to seaweed responding to rolling waves in the ocean. The cochlea is a tiny coil, like a snail shell, and the specialized stereocilia are arranged in the coil like keys on a piano, high to low pitch. When these hair cells move, they convert the hydraulic energy into electrical signals, which are then captured by the auditory nerve. High pitch energy is collected by the stereocilia at the base of the cochlea. Lower pitch energy must travel further through the cochlea to stimulate the stereocilia designated for low sounds. The auditory nerve sends those electrical signals to the brain. Our brain interprets these signals as sound. This process of hearing I just described is called air conduction.

There is another way we perceive sound, and that is through bone conduction. Hearing via bone conduction occurs when the bones in our skull (not the bones in our middle ear) vibrate, which directly stimulates the fluid in the cochlea. Bone conduction hearing does not rely on the outer or middle ear. You may be familiar with bone conduction (or open ear) headphones, which sit firmly next to your ears but not over them. Or you may have heard of a bone anchored hearing aid (BAHA). These devices transmit vibrations directly to the cochlea, activating the stereocilia to send electrical sound signals to the brain.

When you think about the vast diversity of sounds our mouths create in order to produce words, and then imagine each sound transmitted to our brain through the hearing process, it is incredible how sensitive this system must be to perceive the difference between words such as "lake" and "like" or "tart" and "start."

Other Important Structures in the Ear

Other structures in the ear do not participate directly in the process of hearing, but they play important roles as well.

The eustachian tube, which connects the middle ear to the throat, equalizes air pressure and prevents fluid build up in the middle ear, allowing the process of air conduction to occur easily. You might have experienced an ear infection or a "head cold" where your ears felt full and it was more difficult to hear. You have probably felt your ears "pop" when changing altitude in a plane or car created a difference in air pressure. The eustachian tube is responsible for draining fluid from the middle ear when you are sick, and releasing or increasing the air pressure of the middle ear when there is a difference in air pressure around you.

Babies can get middle ear infections easier than adults because their eustachian tubes are shorter and more horizontal, allowing fluid and germs to become trapped. As a child, you might have had tubes placed in your ears. These tiny tubes placed in the eardrum allow any built-up fluid in the middle ear to drain into the ear canal until the eustachian tube grows longer and more vertical, allowing it to properly maintain a dry middle ear cavity.

Connected to the cochlea, the vestibular system consists of the semicircular canals and the vestibular nerve. They are responsible for providing our brain with information about motion, head position, and spatial orientation. The semicircular canals are continuous with the cochlea, meaning there is not a wall that separates the cochlea space and the semicircular canal space, and the fluid (called endolymph) fills both of them. Some people with hearing loss have Meniere's disease, which can be the result of an abnormal amount of fluid in the inner ear. This can cause hearing loss, and also vertigo, or dizziness.

Types of Hearing Loss

There are three types of hearing loss: conductive, sensorineural, and mixed. Keep in mind that the following descriptions of hearing loss are technically dense and full of anatomical terminology. Take it at your own pace, and always feel free to refer back to the information from earlier sections. Remember that these terms may take a while to feel familiar with, especially if these are new to you!

Conductive Hearing Loss

Conductive hearing loss occurs when sound waves do not get through the outer and/or middle ear. Remember, air conduction is perceiving sound via airwaves traveling through the auditory canal, tympanic membrane, and ossicles in the middle ear which activate hydraulic waves in the cochlea. Differences in the shape of the pinna and auditory canal can decrease the acoustic energy of the sound waves that enter your ear. A ruptured or punctured eardrum will not vibrate with the same strength as a healthy eardrum. A fluid-filled middle ear (remember, the middle ear is an air-filled cavity that should remain relatively dry) or misformed ossicles can fail to send strong enough waves via the oval window to activate the stereocilia in the cochlea. Some causes of conductive hearing loss are: frequent middle ear infections, ear wax build up, perforated or malformed eardrum, benign tumors and otosclerosis (abnormal bone growth in the middle ear). Surgery can sometimes improve a conductive hearing loss.

Sensorineural Hearing Loss

Sensorineural hearing loss (SNHL) occurs when the inner ear (cochlea, stereocilia and/or auditory nerve) is not functioning properly. Imagine the tiny hair cells in the cochlea like seaweed, swaying in the ocean as the waves roll over it. These hair cells can become damaged, bent or broken, and they no longer activate the electrical signal to send to the brain. Remember the stereocilia ("seaweed") are arranged along the entire coil of the cochlea. Those that are at the base of the coil are responsible for high pitched sounds, and those toward the center of the coil respond to low pitched sounds. If you have a high frequency sensorineural hearing loss (difficulty hearing high pitches), it is likely the stereocilia at the base of the coil are in some way damaged;

however, you may be able to hear middle and low sounds with ease. One of the most common causes of sensorineural hearing loss is damage to the stereocilia from loud noise. Other causes of sensorineural hearing loss include illness, ototoxic medications, genetics, and the natural aging process. Most of the time, medicine or surgery can not restore hearing caused by issues in the inner ear.

Mixed Hearing Loss

Mixed hearing loss is simply a combination of conductive hearing loss and sensorineural hearing loss.

Noise-Induced Hearing Loss

It is important to be educated about noise-induced hearing loss. Listening to loud music or being exposed to loud machinery can permanently damage the stereocilia in the cochlea. Imagine loud noise creating strong sound waves that travel through your outer and middle ear. The ossicles (tiny bones in the middle ear) vibrate hard, pushing into the oval window to create strong waves in the fluid of the cochlea. If the wave is caused by a sudden, very loud noise such as a gunshot or explosion, the sensitive stereocilia can bend and break under such force. If the wave is caused by loud music repetitively over a period of time, the stereocilia can become overworked and die. Damage to these tiny hair cells is irreversible and will cause permanent hearing loss, and you may not realize it is happening at the time of exposure. The extent of damage depends on how loud the noise is and the amount of time you are exposed. You can avoid causing additional hearing loss by protecting your ears with ear muffs or earplugs when around loud noise, turning down the volume, creating distance between yourself and the source of loud noise, and taking breaks from noise exposure.

Tinnitus

Tinnitus (TIN-ni-tus or tin-NYE-tus) is ringing, buzzing, roaring, hissing, clicking, humming (heard in one or both ears) that are not caused by external sound. It is a common problem for many people with hearing loss. For those of us with sensorineural hearing loss, tinnitus can occur because the stereocilia in the cochlea are bent or damaged. They "leak" random electrical impulses that get sent via the auditory nerve to the brain. Other causes include: ear infections, Meniere's disease, eustachian tube dysfunction, stiffening of the middle ear ossicles (otosclerosis), and muscle spasms in the inner ear. For some people, tinnitus is a serious problem that can cause stress, sleep problems, trouble concentrating, memory problems, depression, anxiety, and irritability. Wearing hearing aids can often help. Talk to your audiologist or otolaryngologist (ENT doctor) for treatment options.

LOCATIONS OF HEARING LOSS
JOURNAL ACTIVITY

Use your art supplies to indicate the location of each type of hearing loss:

conductive hearing loss | sensorineural hearing loss

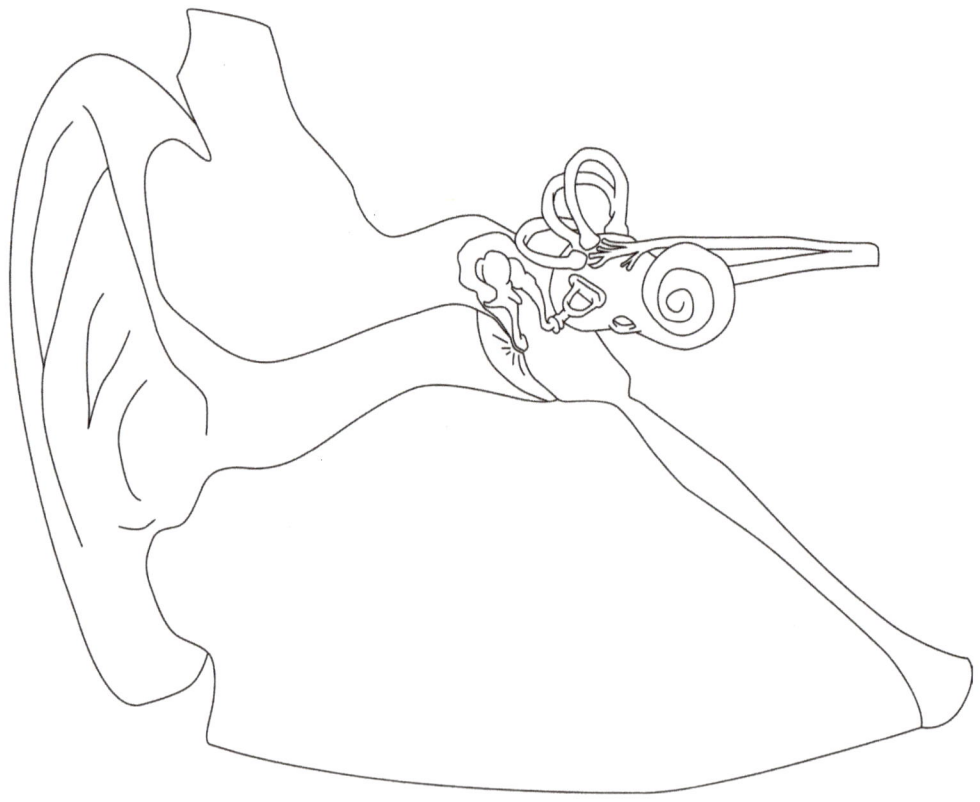

Section Three

Now, let's go over what an audiogram can and can't tell you about your hearing loss. We will also learn about pure tone audiometry and how to read the audiogram graph.

Hearing Testing

When given a hearing test, the audiologist will likely bring you into a soundproof booth. You will go through a variety of tests and be asked to respond when you hear tones, beeps and words played into your left or right ear. An audiogram is a graph, along with other tables and text, showing the results of your hearing test. Because the test is done in a soundproof booth, most of your results represent what you can hear in a perfect listening environment.

It is important to know that even though the audiogram can inform you about the speech sounds that you will have the greatest difficulty hearing, it does NOT inform you of how well you will comprehend speech in noisy everyday environments. The audiogram does not take into account the cognitive effects experienced by d/Deaf and hard of hearing people due to listening fatigue. For a person with hearing loss, there are many factors that go into understanding speech at any given moment, such as proximity to the speaker, prior knowledge of the topic, ability to focus, amount of interfering background noise, cognitive energy spent filling in the blanks, current functioning of hearing devices and assistive technology, and the list goes on. These will be areas we address in upcoming chapters. For now, let's focus on what information an audiogram does provide.

Pure Tone Audiometry

The primary piece of information on your audiogram report is the graph where your hearing thresholds are plotted. This graph consists of an x-axis and y-axis. The x-axis, or horizontal axis that runs from side to side, represents frequency (and is measured in Hertz). The frequency of a sound wave indicates the pitch of a sound, which ranges from low sounds on the left side of the graph to high sounds on the right. The y-axis, or vertical axis that runs from top to bottom, represents hearing level (measured in decibels). Hearing level indicates the loudness or intensity of a sound, ranging from very quiet at the top of the graph to very loud at the bottom. When the audiologist plays a tone at a specific frequency (or pitch) in your ear, they place a mark at the line corresponding to the hearing level where you could just barely hear it. This is called your hearing threshold. This testing process is called pure tone audiometry.

Speech Banana

When the sounds of speech are plotted on the audiogram graph, as shown in this picture, the shape formed looks a bit like a banana, hence the name "speech banana." The purpose of the speech banana helps you understand your audiogram a little better. Remember the marks on the graph are made when you can just barely hear the sound and in a near perfect (silent) environment. The speech sounds located at these frequencies and decibel levels represent the approximate loudness when listening to someone talk in a quiet environment standing 2-3 feet away from you. When background noise and distance occur in real life listening situations, the sounds of speech must be louder in order to be heard, so the speech banana would move lower on the y axis of the audiogram graph.

Audiogram Graph

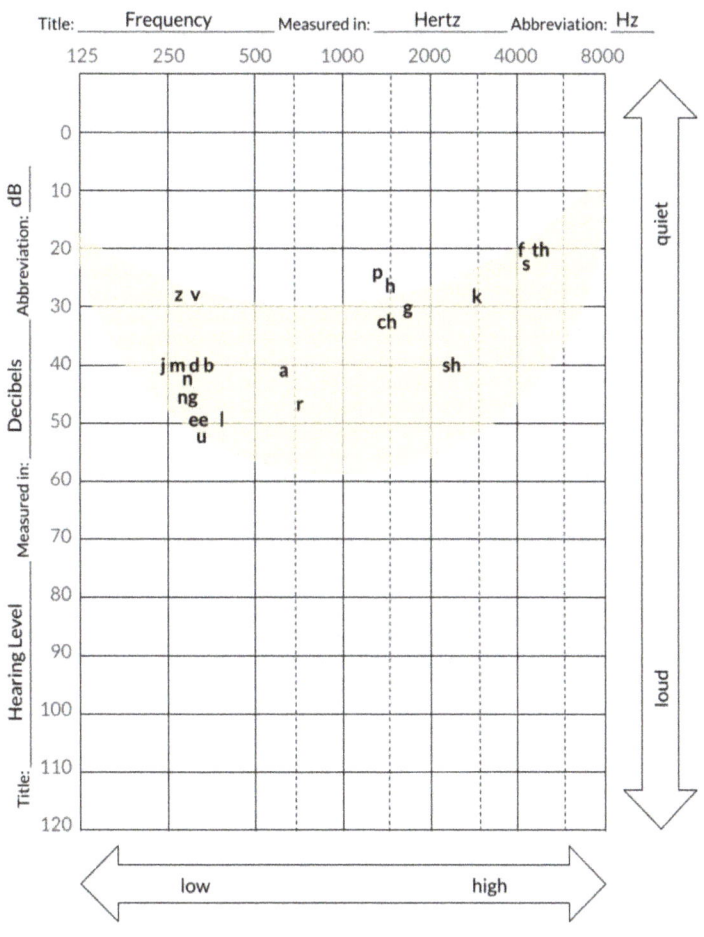

AUDIOGRAM GRAPH-LABELING
JOURNAL ACTIVITY

Label the following elements on the graph:

- titles of the x and y axis including the unit of measure and abbreviation (using the terms frequency, hearing level, hertz, decibels)

- the arrows with the words "low to high" and "loud to soft,"

- these sounds of speech (z, v, j, m, d, b, n, ng, ee, l, u, a, r, p, h, g, ch, sh, k, f, s, th)

Use your creativity to illustrate the important information.

Audiogram Graph-Labeling

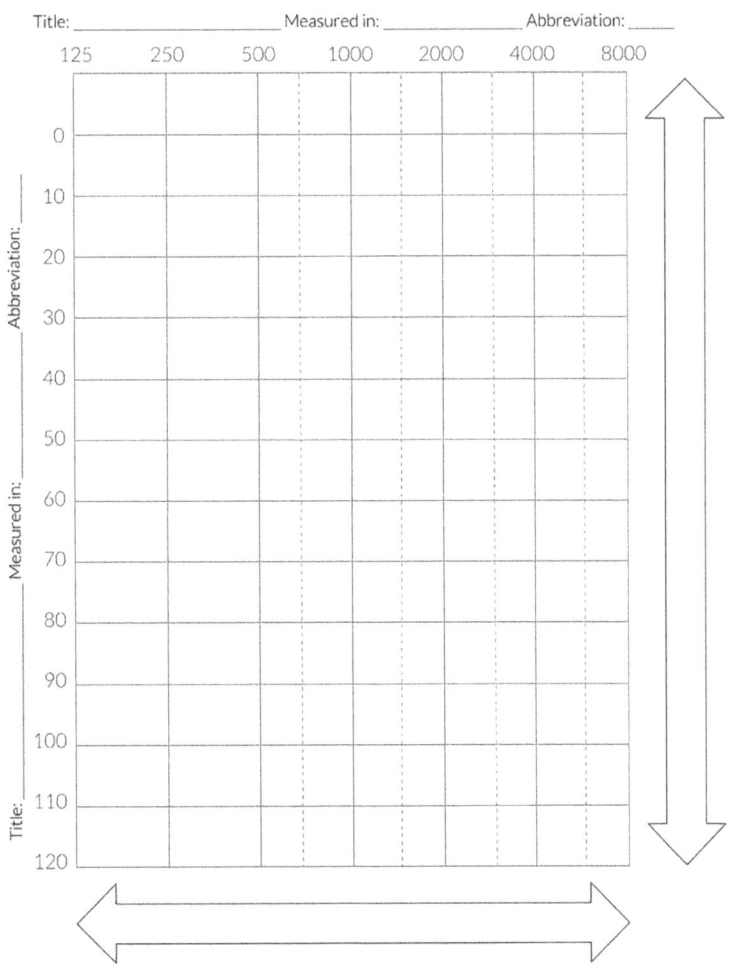

Title: _____ Measured in: _____ Abbreviation: _____

| | 125 | 250 | 500 | 1000 | 2000 | 4000 | 8000 |

Abbreviation: _____

Measured in: _____

Title: _____

0
10
20
30
40
50
60
70
80
90
100
110
120

Section Four

It's time to learn about air conduction testing, bone conduction testing, the purpose of masking, and how this information all gets documented on the audiogram graph.

Air Conduction Testing

Air conduction testing tests conductive hearing. You will wear headphones or earphones for a portion of the test. During this time, the audiologist is testing your hearing using air conduction. Air conduction means the sounds are played into your ear and travel through your ear canal, vibrating the eardrum causing the ossicles to vibrate which in turn creates waves in the fluid in the cochlea, sending electrical signals to the auditory nerve and finally to your brain where you perceive these signals as sound.

Bone Conduction Testing

Bone conduction testing tests the inner ear, or sensorineural hearing. The audiologist will place a tight headband (or bone conductor) over your head with a piece that sits on the bony part (the mastoid bone) located behind your ear. This device delivers sound vibrations directly to the cochlea, bypassing the outer and middle ear entirely. This allows the audiologist to test the hearing sensitivity just in your inner ear.

Masking

Masking is when one ear's cochlea is disengaged, or "kept busy," with white noise so that the other ear's bone conduction can be tested more easily. When testing your hearing, the headphones, ear inserts, or bone conductor placed on the mastoid bone behind one ear can all vibrate the bones in your skull. Because this vibration can be picked up by both your left and right cochleas, your audiologist may also play white noise in one ear while testing the hearing on the other ear. The purpose of this is to keep the cochlea in the non-testing ear busy with noise, so when you respond that you heard a beep, tone or word, it is likely because you heard it in the tested ear.

Marking Symbols

Audiologists use different symbols of varied shape and color to convey your hearing test results. An audiogram symbol key is provided for your reference. Air conduction testing, using headphones or ear inserts, is marked on the graph using four symbols. For unmasked testing, you will see a red circle and blue x. For masked testing, they use a red triangle and blue square. Bone conduction testing, using the bone conductor placed behind the ear, is marked on the graph using 4 different symbols. For unmasked testing, they will use red < and blue > shapes. For masked testing, you will see red [and blue] shapes on your graph. Symbols with a downward arrow are used to show that you didn't hear the sound.

Used less frequently are the symbols: S, A, and CI. S is used to indicate sounds were presented using speakers in the booth rather than directed into one ear only using headphones, ear inserts or the bone conductor. A or CI is used to indicate testing done while wearing a hearing aid (A) or cochlear implant (CI).

When reading the audiogram, keep in mind that for each frequency, any decibel levels above the mark were inaudible during the test.

Audiogram Key		
	Right	Left
Air Conduction	O	X
Air Conduction–Masked	△	□
Bone Conduction	<	>
Bone Conduction–Masked	⊏	⊐
No Response	↙	↘
Soundfield (speakers vs. headphones/bone conductor)	S	
Tested with Hearing Aid	A	A
Tested with Cochlear Implant	CI	CI

PLOT YOUR AUDIOGRAM
JOURNAL ACTIVITY

If you've had your hearing tested, and obtained a copy of your audiogram, use the information provided to plot your audiogram graph in your journal. This will help you focus on the details of your results. If you haven't had your hearing tested yet, there is a sample audiogram in your journal that you can use to practice these skills.

Plot Your Audiogram

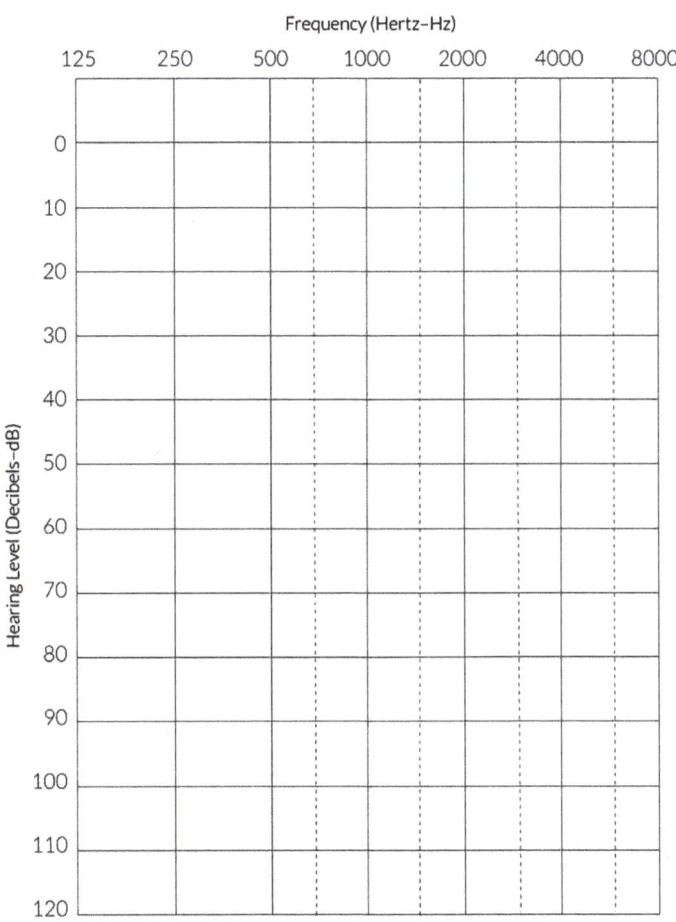

Frequency (Hertz–Hz)

Hearing Level (Decibels–dB)

Section Five

In this section, you will learn how each type of hearing loss (conductive, sensorineural and mixed) shows up on the audiogram graph. You will also learn about pure tone averages and speech discrimination testing.

Types of Hearing Loss

Recall there are three types of hearing loss: conductive, sensorineural and mixed. Based on the audiogram, we can determine the type of hearing loss when we compare air conduction and bone conduction test results. With this information, your audiologist can determine where the cause of your hearing loss exists: the outer/middle ear or the inner ear, or sometimes it can be a combination of both.

Conductive hearing loss will show bone conduction test results as better than air conduction test results. This is often referred to as an air-bone gap. This gap exists because your test results indicate a hearing loss when you were tested using air conduction (earphones or ear inserts that test how well you hear when sound travels through the outer, middle, and inner ear). When you were tested using bone conduction (the tight headband bone conductor that tests how well your inner ear perceives sound), your results are much better than air conduction. This means your difficulty hearing isn't a problem in the cochlea. The problem occurs before it reaches your inner ear.

Sensorineural hearing loss will show relatively the same test results for both air conduction and bone conduction. Here, there will be no air-bone gap. When your hearing was tested using earphones or ear inserts, and sound traveled from the outer ear to the middle ear to the inner ear, a hearing loss was detected. When your hearing was then tested using the bone conductor and sound was delivered directly to the cochlea, the hearing loss detected was virtually the same as it was when testing using air conduction. These results confirm the issue is located in the cochlea.

Mixed hearing loss can show an air-bone gap for some frequencies, but no air-bone gap in other frequencies.

Pure Tone Average (PTA)

The pure tone average (PTA) is a calculation used to estimate how well a person can hear the frequencies used most often in spoken language. It is a shorthand way of describing a hearing loss that doesn't accurately paint the full picture, but it is sometimes used and therefore it is important to understand what it means. The pure tone average is calculated by taking the average hearing threshold levels across 4 frequencies: 500, 1000, 2000, and 4000 Hz. In other words, the PTA is calculated by adding up each of the decibels reported at the listed 4 frequencies, then dividing that total by 4.

For example, when testing using pure tones, if your right ear audiogram looked like this (500 Hz 20 dB, 1000 Hz 35 dB, 2000 Hz 50 dB, 4000 Hz 70 dB), your pure tone average for your right ear would be 20 + 35 + 50 + 70 = 175/4 = 44 dB. This is sometimes used to determine the overall degree of hearing loss in that ear, so 44 dB hearing loss falls into the moderate hearing loss range (we will go over the degrees of hearing loss decibel ranges in the Describing Hearing Loss portion of this chapter).

Speech Discrimination Tests

There are 2 main speech discrimination tests used when you have your hearing tested: speech reception threshold and word recognition.

Speech Reception Threshold (SRT)

The speech reception threshold (SRT) is helpful for understanding the quietest/softest volume at which you can hear and understand a 2-syllable word. The speech reception threshold is obtained by the audiologist asking you to repeat 2 syllable words such as baseball, hotdog, airplane, and bathtub. The softest volume you can repeat these words with 50% accuracy is your speech reception threshold, or SRT. Your speech reception threshold is the decibel level at which you were able to obtain this 50% accuracy score. So, an SRT of 50 dB means that you were able to understand 50% of the words you heard at 50 dB loudness.

Word Recognition Score (WR)

The word recognition score depicts how well you can understand spoken words. The words are presented at sound levels meant to compensate for the frequencies you had difficulty hearing in the pure tone tests. In other words, when you are listening with optimal amplification, are you able to decipher words clearly, or is speech still difficult to understand? The audiologist will say or play a recorded list of single syllable words and have you repeat them. The percentage of accuracy will be your word recognition score. If you were able to accurately repeat 20 of the 25 words, your WR = 80%.

TYPE, PTA, SRT, AND WR
JOURNAL ACTIVITY

Using the information you received on your audiogram, determine your type of hearing loss (conductive, sensorineural, or mixed) for each ear, then calculate your PTA for each ear. Find your Speech Reception Threshold and Word Recognition scores for both ears--they are often different.

	Right	Left
Type of hearing loss		
Pure Tone Average		
Speech Reception Threshold		
Word Recognition		

Reflection: Is any of this information new to you? How does it help you understand how you function with your hearing loss on a day to day basis? If the SRT and WR are missing on your audiogram, decide if you want to request these tests the next time you visit your audiologist.

_____

_____

_____

_____

_____

_____

_____

_____

_____

_____

_____

_____

_____

_____

_____

Section Six

This is the final section of chapter three. We're diving deep into comprehensive hearing loss descriptions, including the five main components often used. And as we close out this rather intensive scientific chapter, we review the purpose of learning about the science of hearing loss, and how this knowledge empowers you to become a more confident self-advocate.

Describing Hearing Loss

The experience of hearing loss is complicated. Many people imagine hearing loss to be a simple change in overall volume, like listening to the radio then turning the volume knob down a few notches. The music sounds the same, except every pitch and note is a little quieter than it was before. If this were the case, hearing aids would act as a simple volume dial and once everything is a little louder, hearing and understanding would be clear. Along the same lines, perhaps the experience of deafness is inaccurately imagined to be the press of a "mute" button on the remote control.

In actuality, hearing loss is complex. If you have a unilateral hearing loss in your right ear, you will have difficulty locating sounds, because you are not hearing sounds from the right side of your head as easily. Functionally, this makes listening during a group discussion difficult if you rely on lipreading but can't locate who is speaking quickly enough.

If you have a high frequency hearing loss and are listening to someone talk, you will likely miss the higher sounds of words (such as /k/, /t/, /s/, /f/, /th/, /sh/, /h/, /wh/) creating an auditory puzzle with pieces missing:

"Wel_ome _o chapter __ree, _earing Lo__ 101, __ere you _ill learn __e ba_i_ __ien_e of _earing lo__. Under__anding _ow __e ear _ork_, _ow _e pro_e_ _ound and _a_ _ar__ of __e ear aren_ _or_ing _ro_erly i_ im_or_an_ in_orma__n _or you _o know."

A more accurate way of describing your hearing loss uses the information provided in your audiogram. Generally, there are five main pieces to a comprehensive hearing loss description: stability, laterality, type, degree, and configuration.

Stability of Hearing Loss

Hearing loss isn't always permanent, and it doesn't always stay the same year after year. We use the following terms to describe the stability of a hearing loss:

- Permanent hearing loss is not expected to change or improve.
- Progressive hearing loss indicates a history of worsening hearing loss, and expected to continue to worsen.
- Fluctuating hearing loss indicates a history of worsening and improving hearing loss over time.
- Stable means hearing levels have not changed based on recent testing.

Laterality of Hearing Loss

We use the terms unilateral and bilateral to describe whether we have hearing loss in one ear (unilateral) or two ears (bilateral.)

Degrees of Hearing Loss

Hearing loss is usually described using a spectrum ranging from slight to profound. Marks are made on the audiogram at the volume (hearing level) measured in decibels (dB), while frequency/pitch is measured in Hertz (Hz). Remember, the marks are made at the hearing level you were just barely able to hear the sound. So, if a 250 Hz (low) sound had to be 60 decibels for you to just barely hear it, the mark goes on the 60dB line. Marks that fall between -10 to 15 dB are in the normal hearing range. Marks that fall between 16 to 25 dB are in the slight hearing loss range. Marks that fall between 26 to 40 dB are in the mild hearing loss range. Marks that fall between 41 to 55 dB are in the moderate hearing loss range. Marks that fall between 56 to 70 dB are in the moderately severe hearing loss range. Marks that fall between 71 to 90 dB are in the severe hearing loss range. Marks that fall below 91 dB are in the profound hearing loss range.

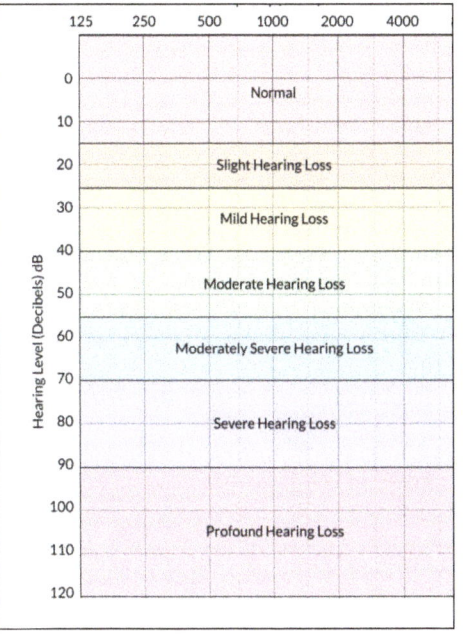

DEGREES OF HEARING LOSS
JOURNAL ACTIVITY

Using your art supplies, shade in different colors the degrees of hearing loss on the graph below. Label them. Use the example on the previous page as a guide, but feel free to unleash your creativity and have fun with this.

-10 to 15 dB = normal hearing

16 to 25 dB = slight hearing loss

26 to 40 dB = mild hearing loss

41 to 55 dB = moderate hearing loss

56 to 70 dB = moderately severe hearing loss

71 to 90 dB = severe hearing loss

Below 91 dB = profound hearing loss

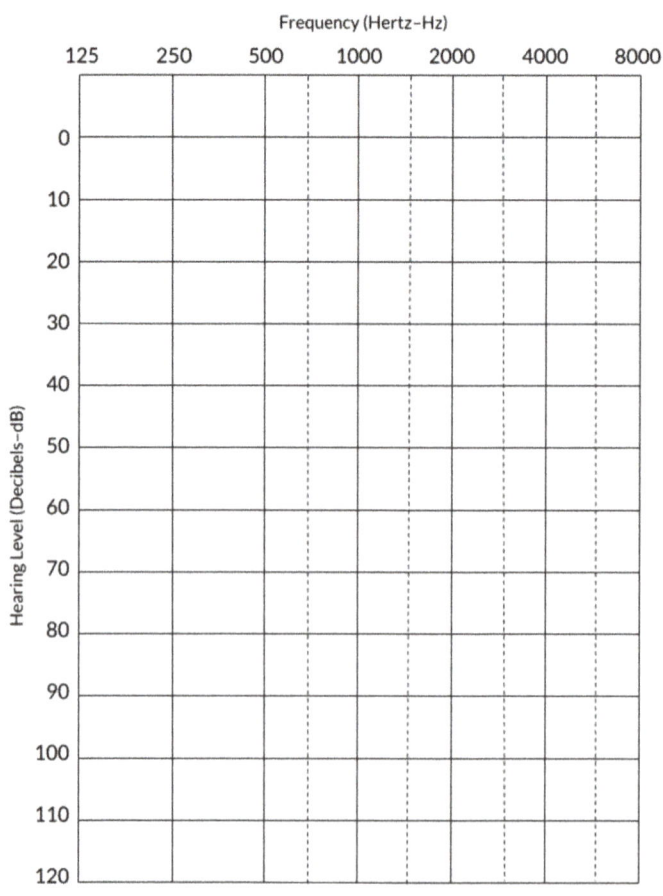

Configuration of Hearing Loss

When a line is drawn connecting the symbols across all the tested frequencies across the audiogram graph, the shape of the line determines the hearing loss configuration. Many people with hearing loss do not have the same degree of hearing loss across all frequencies, and this varies significantly from person to person. The terms most commonly used to describe configuration of hearing loss are: flat, sloping, rising and cookie bite. Let's take a look at how each of these configurations may look on an audiogram.

The flat configuration shows marks across the audiogram at relatively the same decibel level from low frequencies to high frequencies. This means the person has difficulty hearing all frequencies tested at about the same hearing level.

The sloping configuration shows the person hears better in the low frequencies than in the high frequencies.

The rising configuration shows the person has more difficulty hearing in the low frequencies than in the high frequencies.

The cookie bite configuration shows the person has more difficulty hearing in the mid frequencies, and hearing low and high frequencies are relatively easier to hear.

Hearing Loss Descriptions

Using the pieces we just went over, let's put them together to build a more comprehensive hearing loss description.

Here are some sample hearing loss descriptions using these terms:

- I have a progressive unilateral sensorineural mild sloping to severe hearing loss in my right ear.
- I have a permanent bilateral conductive moderate cookie bite hearing loss.
- I have a fluctuating unilateral mixed severe rising to normal limits hearing loss in my left ear.
- I have a permanent bilateral sensorineural flat moderate hearing loss.

In the next journal activity, you will have the opportunity to craft your own hearing loss description in a variety of ways.

"Percentage" of Hearing Loss

You may have heard some people describe their hearing loss with a percentage, i.e. "I am 50% deaf in this ear, and I have 75% hearing in my other ear." This isn't an accurate method of describing hearing loss, and it corresponds to the misconception that hearing loss is simply a turn of the volume dial. Instead of using an inaccurate percentage to describe your hearing loss, you can use what you know from your audiogram to describe how you hear. "I have severe bilateral hearing loss in the mid and high frequencies. This means it is very difficult for me to hear all the sounds of speech even in the best of conditions, but it becomes much more difficult when there is background noise present."

To simplify things, you can also use your PTA (pure tone average) or your WR (word recognition) test score. Examples would be: "I have a 50 dB hearing loss in my right ear and a 75 dB hearing loss in my left ear. I can understand about 65% of speech in good conditions." Keep in mind though, that reducing your description to a single number doesn't accurately represent that you may have much more difficulty hearing high frequencies or that background noise can significantly reduce your ability to understand speech.

DESCRIBE YOUR HEARING LOSS
JOURNAL ACTIVITY

If you have not yet had your hearing test and/or you don't have a copy of your audiogram, practice with the sample audiogram provided on page 32.

Describing your hearing loss is a very personal thing. You may want to be more descriptive with some people, and more simple with others. In chapter five: *Identity & Self-Love*, you will have the opportunity to consider many ways to describe your hearing loss. In this chapter, we are going to apply the more technical aspects used in describing a hearing loss. On page 61, try writing a description of your hearing loss using the following guides:

Comprehensive Description

If your configuration is *rising or sloping*:

I have a [permanent/progressive/fluctuating/stable] [bilateral/unilateral] [sensorineural/conductive/mixed] [degree in low frequencies] [sloping/rising] [degree in mid frequencies] [sloping/rising] [degree in high frequencies] hearing loss.

If your configuration is *flat*:

I have a [permanent/progressive/fluctuating/stable] [bilateral/unilateral] [sensorineural/conductive/mixed] [degree] flat hearing loss.

If your configuration is *cookie bite*:

I have a [permanent/progressive/fluctuating/stable] [bilateral/unilateral] [sensorineural/conductive/mixed] [degree] cookie bite hearing loss.

Pure Tone Average Description

Use the PTA you calculated in the previous journal exercise to write a sentences describing your hearing loss.

- I have a [PTA] decibel hearing loss.
- Example: I have a 50 dB hearing loss.
- I have a [PTA degree of hearing loss] hearing loss.
- Example for a 50 dB PTA: I have a moderate hearing loss.

Word Recognition Score Description

In quiet conditions, I can understand [WR]% speech with my hearing aids/cochlear implant processors.

Describe Your Hearing Loss

Write your descriptions:

_____

_____

_____

_____

_____

_____

_____

_____

_____

How do you feel about these descriptions? If you wrote more than one description, in what situation would you use each of them? Compared to your description(s) you wrote at the start of this chapter, how are these different?

_____

_____

_____

_____

_____

_____

_____

_____

_____

_____

Knowledge is EMPOWERMENT

It is important to have strong background knowledge of the ear anatomy, the process of hearing, how hearing is tested, how to interpret the results of an audiogram and how to technically describe your own hearing.

This knowledge empowers you to:

- Know the next questions to ask your audiologist, otolaryngologist, or Ear, Nose and Throat (ENT) doctor
- Recognize what type of voice might be more difficult to understand (high vs. low)
- Describe to others that hearing loss isn't just "everything is quieter"
- Understand how noise interferes with speech understanding
- Accurately predict what assistive technology may be helpful for you
- Confidently state your accommodation needs in any setting

Remember, your audiologist is the best person to ask about your hearing test results.

4 | the emotional impact of hearing loss

Section One

In this section, we'll start with a journal activity and then go over chapter goals. Next, we will discuss the foundational concepts used in this chapter, and finish out with another journal activity.

First, let's write about your hearing loss and how you feel about it. If you have had hearing loss since childhood, complete the "early onset" writing prompts on page 64. If you've developed hearing loss as an adult, use the "late onset" writing prompts on page 66. Your goal right now is to read the journal prompts and simply write down your thoughts and feelings. Take as much time as you need. Maybe you've never taken the time to consider how you feel about your hearing and how it impacts your life. Remind yourself to be non-judgemental—all of your feelings are valid and deserve space. The time and energy you spend writing today is valuable. We will revisit these journal pages as we move through the exercises in this chapter.

If when completing a journal activity, you find you need more space to write or draw, flip to the back of your journal and use the numbered blank pages there. In the original journal prompt, jot down the page number of the blank page(s) you used so you can easily find where your thoughts are continued at the back of the book.

MY HEARING LOSS: EARLY ONSET
JOURNAL ACTIVITY

Early Onset means your hearing loss was discovered in childhood.

1. How was your hearing loss managed in your family?

2. How was your hearing loss talked about?

3. Did you feel supported at home? If so, how? If not, what do you wish they would have done?

4. Did you feel supported at school? If so, how? If not, what do you wish your teachers would have done?

5. Did your peers know about your hearing loss? If so, did they support you? Tease you? Ignore you?

6. What vivid or specific memories do you have about your hearing loss as a child or teenager?

7. How do you feel your hearing loss has affected your choices in adulthood? Did it impact how you decide who you socialize with? Your romantic relationships? Your job?

8. How do you cope with your hearing loss as an adult?

9. How do you feel about your hearing loss now? Why?

_____
_____
_____
_____
_____
_____
_____
_____
_____
_____
_____
_____

MY HEARING LOSS: LATE ONSET
JOURNAL ACTIVITY

Late Onset means you've developed hearing loss as an adult.

1. Has your hearing loss changed your relationships with the people in your family? How?
2. Has your hearing loss changed your relationships with your friends? How?
3. Has your hearing loss changed your relationships with coworkers? How?
4. Has your hearing loss changed how you do your job? How?
5. Has your hearing loss changed how you socialize? How?
6. Are you mourning the loss of your hearing? What stages are you going through? (5 stages of grief: denial and isolation, anger, bargaining, depression, acceptance)
7. How do you feel about your hearing loss? Why?

_____

_____

_____

_____

_____

_____

_____

_____

_____

_____

_____

_____

_____

_____

_____

_____

Chapter 4 Goals:

- I have thought deeply about my negative experiences with hearing loss and how they impact me emotionally.
- I understand the basics of Cognitive Behavioral Theory and can apply it to my own thinking.
- I can recognize my current thoughts and experiences with hearing loss (no matter if I feel they are negative, neutral, and positive) as valid.
- I can reframe my thoughts, feelings, and behaviors applying a growth mindset and positive assumptions.
- I can define internalized stigma and can recognize its effects on me.
- I can fight internalized stigma using positive imagery to contradict its negative message.
- I have thought deeply about my positive experiences with hearing loss and how they strengthen me.

Introduction

We spent time in chapter one learning about a growth mindset. As a reminder, mindset is an established set of attitudes you hold, and growth mindset is the belief that you have the capacity to grow, change, and develop new skills and attitudes. As you approach the topic of how your hearing loss impacts you emotionally, you will lean heavily on your growth mindset to consider your negative experiences as opportunities to grow. While some of your negative experiences might be things that have been done to you and out of your control, how you respond and how you proactively prepare for future situations is in your control; this is a skill to be developed, and you may not always feel like you are or will be in control of how you respond and prepare.

Additionally, you will apply the principles of cognitive behavioral theory, or CBT, as a way to challenge beliefs that may be holding you back. CBT is the idea that your thoughts, feelings, and behaviors all impact one another; when you're considering mindset, you can understand that your thoughts lead to your feelings, which then lead to your behaviors. Changing the way you think about a situation can significantly improve your chances of a successful experience next time.

It is important that you recognize the emotional impact your hearing loss may have in your life and to honor your feelings as they arise. There may be many positive experiences you've enjoyed because of your hearing loss. Perhaps you have met some wonderful people that have become your close friends because they also have hearing loss, or your hearing loss has influenced your decision to pursue a rewarding career. You have probably also had some impactful negative experiences because of your hearing loss. Hearing loss can create acute frustration during the most pleasant of social gatherings. It can build a solid wall of isolation just when you most need human connection. Hearing loss can well up in a red wave of anger in the midst of watching your favorite movie when the caption timing is off. You may have experienced fear because of your hearing loss: unable to hear someone walking behind you, unable to hear your child calling for you, unable to locate the source of an emergency siren. Hearing loss can escort you down the path of depression when you're exhausted from listening fatigue, feel lost in a sea of conversation and convinced you're doomed to a life of quiet social withdrawal.

Because hearing loss impacts your ability to communicate and participate socially, anger, denial, isolation, fear, fatigue, and sadness are dangerous yet frequently unrecognized side effects of hearing loss. It is absolutely necessary to recognize your feelings, and to give them some time and attention. By labeling these emotions, describing them and examining their origins in this chapter, you will honor and validate your frustrations and struggles. Having given them a place to exist outside of your heart, we will apply your newly developed growth mindset to move forward, and apply CBT allowing new thoughts, experiences and feelings that nurture your sense of well-being and happiness for your future.

Your goal in this chapter is to acknowledge the emotional impact hearing loss has on living your life and how to reframe your thinking. You want to honor past experiences, reframe them with intention, and plan to move forward proactively and assertively.

In chapter seven: *People & Places*, you will dive deeper into the most important relationships in your life and create plans of action toward improving and nurturing them. So as you go through the exercises in this chapter, while you are frequently recalling experiences with those important people, your focus is applying the principles of growth mindset and CBT to reframe how you think about these types of situations.

In chapter eight: *Self Care*, you will consider the frustrations surrounding listening fatigue, advocacy fatigue and audism in depth. These are all emotionally charged topics, and they likely contribute significantly to the negative experiences you have as a person with a hearing disability. While you move through the exercises in this chapter, know that we will address these other important issues with more time and attention in chapter eight.

Some exercises in this chapter may be emotionally difficult. It is important to prepare yourself for this, but please, stay with me. While the big picture of this guided journal is to help you discover an empowered and positive perspective on life with your hearing loss, it is important and necessary to examine the hard reality of how your hearing loss may have negatively impacted your life. If you need to take more than one work session to complete any of the activities, please stop whenever you need, complete your Daily Log including choosing a positive affirmation, and make a commitment to return where you left off next time. If you find you need additional support, please reach out to a loved one or therapist. This is a difficult part of this work but it is necessary to make progress in the future sections.

PROCESSING NEGATIVE EXPERIENCES
JOURNAL ACTIVITY

Review your responses to the prompts in the "My Hearing Loss" journal activity. What negative hearing loss related messages and experiences have you had? Today we are going more in-depth and document experiences and attitudes that have pulled you down because of your hearing loss.

Describe these situations. Include details that answer the questions: Who were you with? What happened? When did it happen? Where did it happen? Why did it happen? What led up to the event? What did you think? How did you feel? How did you respond? Be artistic and let color and shape illustrate what happened, or use bullet points and words to just get it out.

If you need more space to write or draw, flip to the back of your journal and use the numbered blank pages there. In the original journal prompt, jot down the page number of the blank page(s) you used so you can easily find where your thoughts are continued.

_____
_____
_____
_____
_____
_____
_____
_____
_____
_____
_____
_____

NOTE: Plan to return to this *Processing Negative Experiences* portion of your journal at any point to add new experiences or recently recalled memories. We aren't keeping a running list of everything bad that's happened to you because of your hearing loss for you to dwell on or relive them. Instead, we are placing them here, for safekeeping outside of your mind and your heart, and for reflection as we reframe your life for more positive experiences.

Give yourself permission to be angry and hurt. You've carried some of that for a long time. While we are not going to dwell very long on these experiences, it is important to give them some space because they have shaped some of your beliefs and actions. Take a minute to reflect on them, close your eyes, take a few slow breaths, and then turn the page. Literally.

Section Two

In this section, you will learn and experience the basic concepts behind Cognitive Behavioral Theory.

Cognitive Behavioral Theory

Cognitive Behavioral Theory suggests that when you have an experience, your THOUGHTS lead to your FEELINGS, which then lead to your BEHAVIORS. Considering your past experiences, what you thought about them, how they made you feel, and the ways in which you responded to your feelings is important in making changes to your future. If you can change how you think about these experiences, you can adjust your emotional response to them, and how you behave because of them.

Situation: When someone said, "nevermind" when you missed a joke, you had thoughts about that. You formed ideas about why they said it and what they were thinking when they said it.

THOUGHTS: They can't be bothered to repeat it. I'm not important to them. They must think I'm too stupid to understand. They just don't get it.

FEELINGS: Rejection, left out, lonely, embarrassed, discounted, invalid.

BEHAVIORS: Stop asking people to repeat something I missed. Just smile and nod. Avoid hanging out with them. Withhold my contributions to the conversation.

Let's apply some growth mindset principles to the thoughts you might have about this interaction in the future. Growth mindset for yourself assumes you have the capacity to learn and to change. Growth mindset for others can make the same assumptions: they have the capacity to learn and to change. One of the most powerful words to use when thinking about growth mindset is "yet." Let's look at this situation again, and apply what you know about the growth mindset.

Situation: Someone says, "nevermind" when you missed a joke and everyone else is laughing.

THOUGHTS: That person might not know I have a hearing loss. That person might not understand how hurtful hearing "nevermind" is to me. That person has no idea this happens to me all the time. That person doesn't understand *yet*.

FEELINGS: You very well may still feel left out and discounted, but these new thoughts might also make you feel that this situation could be more about them than it is about you. Perhaps this person is a new friend, and you might feel hopeful that they may be willing and able to understand your perspective. You might feel empowered because instead of withdrawing from conversations in the future, you see an opening for growth.

BEHAVIORS: Maybe you say right then and there, "actually, could you please not say 'nevermind' to me?" Or maybe you choose a later time to talk to this person. You might say, "My hearing loss causes me to miss things, and when you say, 'nevermind' it takes away my ability to decide what is important and what isn't important to understand." You might say, "You might not realize this, but when people used to say that to me, I would withdraw and avoid being social. I enjoy being around you and I want you to understand what I need so we can communicate better."

In this scenario, you have taken a proactive position and are advocating for yourself. You don't have control over how they will respond to these actions, but, instead of smiling and nodding or withdrawing socially, both of which leaves you feeling left out, there are now options on the table with this person. You might have just opened the door to a great conversation with someone who becomes your biggest advocate.

When you have thoughts about a situation, you have many choices. Your thoughts can change quite easily when you adjust your perspective.

You may have negative or irrational thoughts about a situation if you are tired or hungry, or have found yourself in this same situation over and over. Your first thoughts may come from a fixed mindset: "This always happens to me, I must be the cause." "Hearing people will never understand what it's like to be deaf." "Why do I even try?"

It is possible to have positive thoughts about the same situation. You can make a choice to change your perspective, and think using a growth mindset: "This happens to me frequently. I wonder if I try a different approach or use a new strategy, will the outcome be better?" "Many hearing people haven't had the opportunity to know someone who is deaf, so it's difficult for them to be empathetic." "I can be an agent of change."

COGNITIVE BEHAVIORAL
THEORY ILLUSTRATED
JOURNAL ACTIVITY

To help you think a little deeper about this concept, use your creative tools to draw in arrows connecting the words: Thoughts > Feelings > Behaviors. In the space BELOW the word "Thoughts," portray all kinds of random *negative and irrational thoughts* using words and/or images. Move to the space BELOW the words "Feelings" and illustrate the feelings that may come from the negative thoughts. Do the same for "Behaviors." What behaviors might you have when you have those negative feelings?

Then do the same thing above the words, only this time fill the space ABOVE the word "Thoughts" with all kinds of *positive assumptions and open minded thoughts.* Color and draw images ABOVE the words "feelings" and "behaviors" illustrating how those thoughts influence your feelings and behaviors.

Notice how significantly thoughts influence feelings and behaviors. And notice how shifting negative or irrational thoughts with positive rational thoughts can profoundly change your feelings and your behaviors.

If you need to see an example of a completed journal entry for this activity, see page 80.

Thoughts   Feelings   Behaviors

If they know I have a hearing loss, they will want to help.

People are used to a fast pace — they will appreciate slowing down!

People have a lot on their mind — it's easy to forget I have a hearing loss.

People will appreciate being reminded — those people that love me.

People want to help — they don't know how yet.

- Hopeful.
- Confident.
- Encouraged.
- Understanding.
- Patient.
- Supported.
- EMPOWERED.
- Proud.
- Unashamed.
- LOVED.
- Reinforced.
- Mindful.

- Quick to remind people.
- Live in the moment → mindful communication.
- Speak up — once, twice OFTEN!
- Advocate more often.
- Support others.
- Have more energy for other activities.
- Engage.
- Provide positive feedback and appreciation !!

Thoughts ➡ Feelings ➡ Behaviors

- Most people don't care.
- No one wants to help me.
- Everyone is grumpy & impatient.
- People don't think enough about what I need. (I'm always thinking about what THEY need.)
- If they know I have a hearing loss, they will think I'm dumb / incapable / a burden.

- SAD
- Left out.
- Lonely
- Angry!
- Forgotten
- Less than.
- HURT
- Neglected. Ignored.
- Looked down on.
- LOST
- Disrespected.

- Withdraw.
- Distract myself from the activity / conversation / feelings.
- Wait for someone to notice.
- Stop caring about what the other person needs.
- Don't give eye contact.
- Leave.
- Yell, cry, storm out.
- Just sit here.
- Pretend / Bluff.
- Snap back.

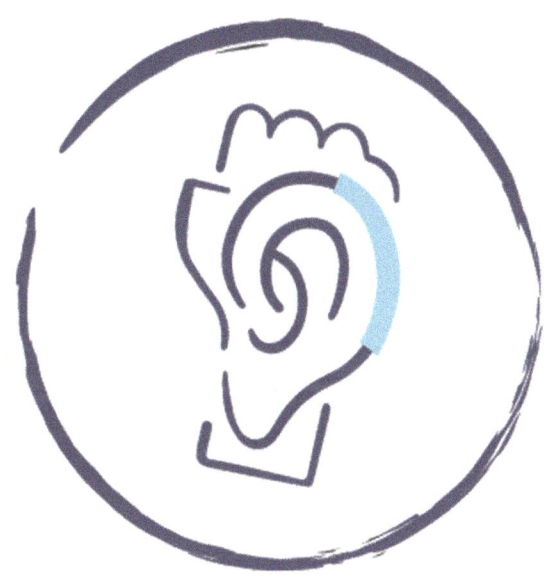

Section Three

In this section, you will practice applying Cognitive Behavioral Theory (CBT) to a scenario and begin to consider how this practice can be applied to living an empowered life with hearing loss.

CBT Practice

Today you will practice applying CBT to a common situation you may have experienced.

Our situation today is set in a grocery store. You have gathered all the items on your list and are about to check out. When the clerk says something you can't understand, you simply ask them to repeat what they said. To your embarrassment and your surprise, the grocery clerk practically shouts at you, "How are you? Did you find everything you needed?"

What thoughts pop into your mind? Perhaps it goes something like this: That person is so rude! People are turning their heads to look at me. They probably think I'm dumb. This always happens to me.

Feelings that arise from those thoughts might be: Embarrassment, anger, humiliation, defeat, and strong desire to never shop here again!

Possible behaviors that sprout from those feelings could be: Duck your head and hope people don't notice your face turning red. Mumble an apology, pay for your groceries and hurry out. In the future, look for the self checkout to avoid interacting with clerks. And, maybe you internalize feelings of shame about your hearing loss.

COGNITIVE BEHAVIORAL THEORY PRACTICE
JOURNAL ACTIVITY

After considering the first scenario with the grocery clerk, and noticing how the thoughts dictated the feelings and then the behaviors, consider new ways to think about the situation. What happens when you assume the shouting isn't because of you, but rather about that clerk having a bad day? Or what happens when you think the clerk has a relative with hearing loss and that's how they talk to them when they don't hear? The skeptic in you may be thinking, "but what if the clerk was actually just being a jerk?" Perhaps that's true, but the important part of this activity is to ASSUME something positive to observe how it impacts your feelings and actions. Based on positive thoughts, now observe how your feelings are different from the first scenario. And finally, what might you DO differently BECAUSE of those feelings?

Situation: The grocery clerk shouts at me when I asked them to repeat what they said.

THOUGHTS: _____
_____
_____

FEELINGS: _____
_____
_____

BEHAVIORS: _____
_____
_____

Section Four

In this section, we are going to work in your journal to reclaim and reframe some of those negative experiences you wrote about at the beginning of this chapter.

RECLAIMING AND REFRAMING
JOURNAL ACTIVITY

Now, look back to the Processing Negative Experiences activity on pages 71-73. Circle 2-3 situations that have stuck with you. These may be experiences that have made it difficult for you to feel confident and happy, or experiences that could use a new perspective. Choose one for now.

Turn ahead to page 86 to find the first Reclaiming and Reframing journal page. Write that negative experience at the bottom of the page. Can you describe your THOUGHTS during this experience? What about your FEELINGS? How did you feel during and after this experience? Finally, what did you do because of this experience? How have your BEHAVIORS changed the way you've lived life since this happened? Write all of these thoughts, feelings and behaviors along the bottom half of the page.

Up until today, the memory of this experience has hindered your self-image as a person with hearing loss. However, this is something that has happened in the past, and you are focused on the future. As you consider this experience, begin to color in the letters and the spaces around your written words with brown, black, and gray. As you color, imagine you are laying the image of this experience into the ground and covering it with rich earthy soil. As you bury the experience, begin to think about your hopes and dreams for your future and living a life without the burden of the negative energy of this memory. We are not erasing the fact that this happened to you, but we are planting it in a quiet corner where we will nurture new growth from it.

Next, applying the concepts of a growth mindset, what new thoughts might you have if this happens again? Are there new ways to think about the experience that might change how you feel about it? We are going to actively reframe this experience with new thoughts. Using your more vibrant shades of red, green, yellow, and purple, write those new thoughts in the space above the fresh soil you used to plant your negative experience.

How do these new thoughts make you feel? If you find yourself in this situation again, how do you imagine yourself feeling based on your new way of thinking about it? What will you do? How will your behavior be an expression of your strength? Of your courage? Of your hope for something different and better?

Use your creativity to build something brand new and beautiful sprouting from the soil (maybe these are flowers, plants, trees, a mandela, rainbow, colorful words, or other random pleasing shapes). Allow yourself to distance from the negative experience and enjoy the process of creating something you hadn't ever imagined could come from this experience. Write words that feel powerful, confident and hopeful. Enjoy this process today and know that while this was not an easy task, you have proven to yourself that even from painful experiences you can rise with renewed energy, perspective and celebration.

If you need to see an example of a completed journal entry for this activity, see page 92.

Reclaiming and Reframing

EXPERIENCE: _____

THOUGHTS: _____
_____
_____

FEELINGS: _____
_____
_____

BEHAVIORS: _____
_____
_____

Reflection: How did it feel to complete this exercise today? Are you able to imagine yourself reconstructing negative thoughts to open minded positive thoughts in future difficult situations related to your hearing loss?

_____

_____

_____

_____

_____

_____

_____

_____

_____

_____

_____

_____

_____

_____

_____

_____

_____

_____

_____

_____

_____

_____

Plan to return and complete the other 2 circled situations from your _Negative Experiences_ on the following pages. If you like, you can do them both before moving on to the next exercise in this chapter. Or you may want to schedule them in a few days when you feel refreshed.

Reclaiming and Reframing

EXPERIENCE: _____

THOUGHTS: _____

_____

_____

FEELINGS: _____

_____

_____

BEHAVIORS: _____

_____

_____

Reflection: How did it feel to complete this exercise today? Are you able to imagine yourself reconstructing negative thoughts to open minded positive thoughts in future difficult situations related to your hearing loss?

_____

_____

_____

_____

_____

_____

_____

_____

_____

_____

_____

_____

_____

_____

_____

_____

_____

_____

_____

_____

_____

_____

Reclaiming and Reframing

EXPERIENCE: _____

THOUGHTS: _____
_____
_____

FEELINGS: _____
_____
_____

BEHAVIORS: _____
_____
_____

Reflection: How did it feel to complete this exercise today? Are you able to imagine yourself reconstructing negative thoughts to open minded positive thoughts in future difficult situations related to your hearing loss?

_____

_____

_____

_____

_____

_____

_____

_____

_____

_____

_____

_____

_____

_____

_____

_____

_____

_____

_____

PRIDE
Self-Respect
VOICE
BRAVE
Empowered
Important

Reclaiming and Reframing

What he did had nothing to do with me.

The class knew he was a jerk.

He needed me to push back so that he knew he was wrong.

Other students would benefit from me being a role model.

My understanding MATTERS!

I deserved to learn like everyone else in the class!

EXPERIENCE: My college professor mocked me in class.

THOUGHTS: He is so mean. He wants to humiliate me in front of everyone. I'm an idiot for speaking up. Everyone thinks I'm annoying and self-centered. I asked for too much

FEELINGS: Embarrassed! Ashamed. My understanding is not important. Insignificant. Alone. Humiliated. Angry! UNSAFE! At a disadvantage.

BEHAVIORS: Stop asking for what I need. Stop talking and stop participating. Sit toward the back. Avoid seeing or talking to him. Avoid future professors!

Section Five

In this final section of chapter four you will learn about internalized stigma about hearing loss and practice how to take away its limiting power over you. You will also have the opportunity to consider the positive experiences you've had because of your hearing loss.

Internalized Stigma

Internalized stigma occurs when a person with hearing loss cognitively or emotionally absorbs negative messages or stereotypes about hearing loss and comes to believe them as true.

There are countless negative images and messages associated with hearing loss in our culture today. We must recognize that those images and messages have infiltrated our minds and have influenced how we feel about ourselves and our hearing loss.

What are the messages that hold you back? When you know it is important to inform someone about your hearing loss, and you just can't bring yourself to do it, what prevents you? If you feel shame or embarrassment, are there negative images or messages that feed those emotions?

Our society, and even the hearing technology industry, reinforces the stigma of hearing loss. "It's practically invisible!" "No one will know you are wearing it."

INTERNALIZED STIGMA
JOURNAL ACTIVITY

For this exercise, think of three negative messages about hearing loss you've heard from others in your life, from the media, or just by living in the world. Here are some examples to choose from, or come up with your own.

Only old people have hearing loss.

People with hearing disabilities are not as smart as hearing people.

Hearing aids/Cochlear implants make people look weak.

People assume deaf people can't _____.

Asking for accommodations is embarrassing.

Write one statement in the center of the circle. Do the same for the other two statements on the following two pages.

Next, in the space all around each of the negative messages, write and draw and express all kinds of positive statements and images that contradict the negative message. If the negative message is weakness or embarrassment, use descriptive language or images and color that boldly express strength and assertiveness. If the negative statement is inability, focus on ability. If the negative statement is derogatory toward age (ageism), portray strength, wisdom and vibrancy of the heart and mind regardless of physical age.

If you need to see an example of a completed journal entry for this activity, see page 99.

Internalized Stigma

Internalized Stigma

Internalized Stigma

Internalized Stigma

Reflection: How did it feel to complete this exercise? Did this process change your feelings about the stigma of hearing loss? How?

_____

_____

_____

_____

_____

_____

_____

_____

_____

_____

_____

_____

_____

_____

_____

_____

_____

_____

_____

_____

_____

_____

Internalized Stigma

If I have the accommodation, I will have more energy later in the day to enjoy doing something for ME!

I'm not the only one!

I can be an example to others.

Someone else might need the same accommodation.

What if the accommodation doesn't work?

Asking today makes it easier to ask tomorrow.

Because I can hear with the accommodation, I can understand. I can participate.

• TIRED!

People will judge me as "less than"

Asking for accommodations is EMBARRASSING

No one else has to

What if they refuse?

Calls attention to myself

I'm worth it. My understanding is important!

I'm letting others know how to treat me.

People will have an opinion about me if I DON'T understand what's going on. I'd rather their opinion be about me understanding and participating.

POSITIVE EXPERIENCES
JOURNAL ACTIVITY

You have done a lot of difficult work considering some of the most difficult times of your life and practicing ways to reframe them into something useful for your future. Now, you are going to celebrate the positive experiences you've had because of your hearing loss.

Describe times in your life when your hearing loss contributed something positive. Maybe it allowed you to meet certain people you wouldn't have met otherwise. What are your great examples of when you demonstrated courage or determination? Have you been able to positively influence someone else? Write it, draw it, celebrate it!

_____

_____

_____

_____

_____

_____

_____

_____

_____

_____

_____

_____

_____

_____

_____

Positive Experiences

_____
_____
_____
_____
_____
_____
_____
_____
_____
_____
_____

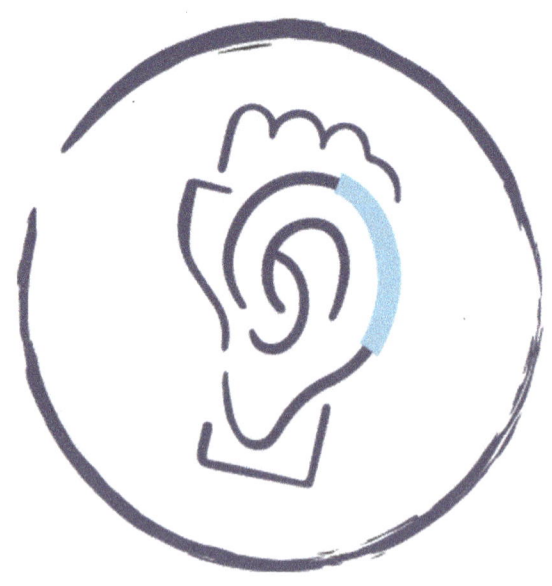

5 | identity & self-love

Section One

Welcome to chapter five: Identity & Self-Love. In this section, we'll go over the goals for this chapter. Next, we will discuss the foundational concepts for this chapter, consider where you stand on the continuum of acceptance, and finish out with a journal activity.

Chapter 5 Goals:
- I can describe the difference between denial and acceptance and can identify where I currently am on this continuum.
- I understand the many words and labels people use for hearing loss and can describe how they are different.
- I am prepared to disclose my hearing loss clearly and effectively in different situations.
- My identity includes my hearing loss identity.
- I know how to find others in the Deaf and Hard of Hearing community.
- I can describe the difference between introvert and extrovert and can identify where I naturally fit on this continuum.

- I have considered how my hearing loss may influence how I interact socially.
- I have explored how stigma can influence my feelings about hearing technology.

Introduction

Whether you have had your hearing loss since childhood, or have developed it later in life, you may be struggling with fully accepting it. It is actually pretty common for someone with a hearing loss to deny it to others, and also sometimes themselves. Negative experiences and internalized stigma create shame and embarrassment about something that is completely out of your control. The work you did in earlier chapters is the foundation for combating the influence of stigma on a day to day basis. As you continue to work through those emotions, you must also consider how your hearing loss impacts your identity and how you feel about yourself.

Hearing loss is a unique kind of disability because it directly impacts the people with whom we communicate. The hearing world we live in is fast-paced and impatient. There is an unspoken expectation among hearing folks (people that do not have hearing loss) that daily interchanges at work, at the grocery store, and in your home be quick, invisible and effective. Spoken languages are filled with slang, dialect, idioms and imperfectly produced words formed by the mumbly, often-obscured mouths of humans multitasking as they walk, eat, drink, and brush their teeth. Any degree of hearing loss significantly impacts the ability to understand speech in noise, and our world is defined by noise.

As you interact in this world, your ability to understand what someone is saying is only partially in your control. You may have state of the art hearing technology and be an expert at lipreading, but if your communication partner does not make some adjustments to how they communicate, breakdowns occur. Herein lies the bridge that only we can extend: "I have a hearing loss…" "I am deaf…" "I can't hear you…"

Whether you actually offer that information or not, your hearing loss is an important part of your identity. That person with whom you are communicating sees a flag pop up, and either identifies you as someone who happens to have a hearing loss because you told them, or someone who has "something" going on that makes communicating difficult. This isn't always malicious; it's a quick calculation their mind makes when the intricate flow of verbal communication breaks down. This is where you may feel offended when people assume you're not smart. Or feel ignored when they don't continue the conversation. Now don't get me wrong. Some people can just behave in offensive and rude ways that have nothing to do with you. But most of the time, interactions where one or more people have a hearing loss can naturally veer toward the ditch.

This is where you hold the steering wheel. You can smile, nod, and pretend to understand as you let the conversation rumble along in the field, or you can take control by telling your passenger what you need. But that's not the end goal. You alone are not responsible for keeping the conversation on the road and driving through the night. Maybe your communication partner only knows how to drive an automatic, so they need to learn how to operate a stick shift. A little clunky at first, but they're capable. What I mean here is that, yes, disclosure of your hearing loss is your job. Telling people what is helpful (seeing their face, clearer speech, slowing down, repeating, etc) is your job. But after that, there is shared responsibility. We'll go deeper on this shared responsibility in chapter 7: People and Places.

Self-disclosure of a hearing loss is difficult. It is not a "one and done" kind of thing. It is a repetitive, multiple times a day kind of thing. Unless your hearing technology is easily visible, hearing loss is an invisible disability. This became even more obvious during the COVID-19 pandemic when suddenly masks covered mouths everywhere. We lost access to the only visible part of spoken communication–lipreading. People who could once get by with lipreading suddenly encountered barrier after barrier, and self-disclosure of their hearing loss became necessary. We started wearing buttons stating, "I lip read!" or masks with words, "Hard of Hearing, please speak up!" This desire to make an invisible disability visible came from disclosure fatigue. We were tired of telling every single person we spoke with that we couldn't understand them. Giving people that bit of information before the first word was spoken made the interaction a little easier and a little less exhausting.

Your identity includes your hearing loss. Self-disclosure improves communication. When you self-advocate, you feel stronger and more confident. In this chapter, you will become comfortable with the words you use to identify yourself, and discover that you belong to a greater community. You will explore your natural tendencies to be either an extravert or an introvert, and consider how your hearing loss lives alongside your personality. You will practice self-acceptance, and continue to transform "impairment" to empowerment.

Denial vs Acceptance

How do you feel about your hearing loss? Flip back to the journal activity titled My Hearing Loss (page 64 or 66). Reread what you wrote. Where were you in terms of accepting or denying your hearing loss when you wrote that? Where are you today?

Perhaps because you are working through the activities in this book, you have accepted your hearing loss and are ready to move forward. Or maybe someone suggested this book for you and you still prefer to think you don't have a hearing loss. Wherever you are on the continuum of denial to acceptance, the truth is, we probably all vary where we land on any given day. It likely depends on who you're talking to and what kind of listening environment you are in. You might have accepted your hearing loss at home but are not quite ready to tell people at work.

Regardless, you are where you are, and that's OK. Our goal in this work is for you to think deeper about your hearing loss and how it impacts your happiness and your ability to connect to the people you love. Learning about communication strategies and accommodations is only helpful if you are able to use them when you need them. If denial is holding you back, I invite you to consider the value of acceptance.

Acceptance is a form of self-love and empowerment. Self-acceptance is the unconditional acceptance of all of you, the positive and the negative. Acceptance is not defeat–it is simply acknowledgement.

THE ACCEPTANCE CONTINUUM
JOURNAL ACTIVITY

Take a few moments to write your thoughts and feelings about where you are on the continuum of acceptance. Can you identify why you are there? Where do you want to be? What do you need to get you there?

_____

_____

_____

_____

_____

_____

_____

_____

_____

_____

_____

_____

_____

_____

_____

_____

_____

_____

Section Two

In this section, first you'll complete a journal activity. Then we will go over the common phrases and labels often used to describe people with hearing loss. Next we'll discuss why words are powerful and consider the words we choose to use when we talk about our hearing loss.

WORDS
JOURNAL ACTIVITY

The word(s) you use to identify your hearing loss is a very personal choice. How you describe your hearing loss, how it defines you, how it shows up in your identity...that may take some time to process. To start, circle or jot down all the words you have used in the past to describe your hearing loss.

I am...

hearing impaired	hard of hearing	a person with hearing loss
deaf	Deaf	a little bit deaf
half deaf	deafblind	late deafened
oral-deaf		

_____

_____

_____

_____

_____

_____

_____

_____

If you've used more than one, go back and circle your most used phrase.

Reflection: How do you feel when you say the words "I am _____?"

Say this outloud and then honestly reflect on how the words make you feel.

_____

_____

_____

_____

_____

_____

_____

_____

_____

_____

_____

_____

_____

_____

_____

_____

_____

_____

_____

_____

_____

_____

_____

_____

_____

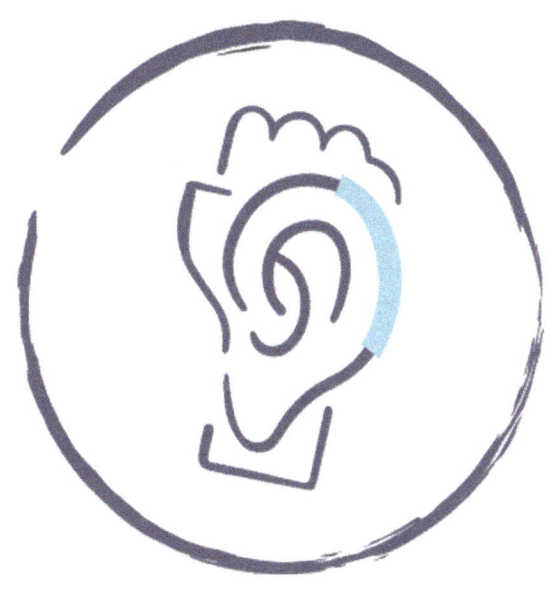

Understanding Common Phrases and Labels

We're going to discuss common words and labels people use to describe hearing loss, looking at both their literal meaning and how the words have been used in the d/Deaf and Hard of Hearing community.

Hearing Impaired, Hearing Impairment

The terms "hearing impaired" and "hearing impairment" are frequently used in the medical, legal, and educational fields, and they usually are used as an umbrella term under which all degrees of hearing loss fit. Literally, it means "not able to hear well." Merriam-Webster defines "impaired" as "being in an imperfect or weakened state or condition: such as diminished in function or ability," and this statement is actually true for the physical condition of the hearing anatomy; however, many deaf and hard of hearing people consider the term "hearing impaired" offensive because the words "imperfect" and "weakened" applied to the person are inaccurate.

Hard of Hearing

"Hard of hearing" is a widely preferred way to identify someone with hearing loss. Generally, "hard of hearing" refers to having a "defective but functional" sense of hearing. This usually means mild to moderate or moderately severe hearing loss that makes understanding speech difficult, but still possible with any number of supports, including technology and/or accommodations.

Hearing Loss

I've been using this term widely as an umbrella label that encompasses all levels of hearing loss, from slight to profound; however, it does have some negative connotations that are important to mention. The word "loss" generally refers to having lost something, and for those of us who acquired hearing loss later in life, it may feel like a good fit. But for those born with diminished or inability to hear, nothing was lost because you can't lose something you never had. "Loss" can also be a word that indicates deficiency. So for those reasons, "hearing loss" is not always preferred. Still, there are not yet other widely understood options to replace it.

Hearing Disabled, Hearing Disability

Similar to the rejection of "impairment," there has been negative feelings about using the word "disability" to describe hearing loss. "Disability" indicates the inability to do major activities of daily living. Especially for those in the Deaf community that use signed language, there really is nothing a Deaf person can't do, except hear. With sign language and new technology, they argue there isn't a necessity to be able to actually hear.

However, many people in the wider disabled community are speaking out about living life with disabilities, and are reclaiming the use of "disabled" and "disability" as appropriate, and even preferred. They have challenged ableism by refusing to hide or be shamed by stigma that used to be associated with those terms. One reason is because the word disability connects people to a larger group, many of whom are advocating for accessibility in one way or another. "Disability" and "individuals with disabilities" are the terms used in the (US) laws written to protect rights and provide equal access.

deaf (also known as "little d" deaf)

The term "deaf" is frequently used and is considered a preferred label in the d/Deaf and Hard of Hearing community. The medical, legal and educational communities tend to define "deaf" or "deafness" as a hearing impairment so severe, with or without amplification, that speech understanding is very poor. So, in general, people with severe to profound hearing loss in most frequencies. The general population also widely views "deaf" to mean literal inability to hear.

However, in recent years, "deaf" is being used as an all-inclusive term for all levels of hearing loss, including deaf, hard of hearing and deafblind. It is not yet widely recognised in general society, and so people may be confused when what they understand to be a "hard of hearing" person uses "deaf" as an identifying label.

Oral-deaf

Oral-deaf is often used to convey the experience of severe to profound hearing loss and that the person uses spoken language, as opposed to signed language, to communicate.

Deaf (also known as "big d" Deaf)

"Deaf" with a capital D is widely recognized to describe the community of people who use signed languages and participate as members of the Deaf community. American Sign Language, British Sign Language and many others are complex and full languages, and those that use them have a rich and deep culture, created by close relationships within the community, complete with history and traditions. It is possible for a person with mild to moderate hearing loss to identify as Deaf if they actively participate in the Deaf community, and for a person with severe to profound hearing loss who doesn't use sign language and primarily functions in the hearing world to identify as hard of hearing or oral-deaf.

Acquired Deafness, Late-Deafened, Sudden Deafness, Sudden Hearing Loss (SHL), Sudden Sensorineural Hearing Loss (SSHL)

These terms are frequently used to describe loss of hearing that occured or developed some time during the lifespan, but it was not present at birth. This is a significant distinction, because someone who was living in the hearing world, using spoken language, loses their ability to hear and is faced with serious, devastating communication challenges. When a hearing loss occurs rapidly, it is considered sudden hearing loss or sudden deafness.

Congenital Deafness

Hearing loss that is present from birth and may or may not be hereditary. A child born hard of hearing or deaf is often provided with early interventions and supported with extra services in K-12 school. For some children, they learn sign language at an early age at home and/or school.

Outdated Terms

Hearing Handicap, Hearing Disorder, Hearing Deficit, Hearing Defect, Hearing Abnormality, Deaf and Dumb, Deaf-Mute

These terms are generally considered outdated and can be seen as offensive. It is important to recognize the history of labels for the deaf, many of which have been harmful or inaccurate. "Dumb" is a multi-meaning word that means "lacking intelligence" and it also means "mute" or "lacking the ability to speak." During the early 19th century, deaf and "dumb" was a widely used descriptor for a person unable to speak, but by the end of the 20th century, the offensiveness of dumb was widely recognized. The people of the Deaf community continue to fight for recognition as highly capable and intelligent with a complex language and culture, and we need to be aware of the power of words and labels.

Person-First Language and Identity-First Language

There is debate in the disabled community about person-first and identity-first language. Person-first language describes the person, then the disability:

A person with a hearing disability.

A person who is deaf.

I have a hearing disability.

Identity-first language describes the disability as part of the person:

A hearing disabled person.

A deaf person.

I am hearing disabled.

Person-first language was once considered the politically correct preference. Its intention was to demonstrate that a person is a person before their disability or diagnosis. However, disabled people began to reject this way of referring to themselves. Having a disability is different from having a medical illness, and person-first language treats having a disability like having an ailment or disease.

I have COVID-19.

I have cancer.

I have a hearing impairment.

While disabilities are diagnosed, they are not the same as an illness because the disability isn't something to be cured nor is it contagious. A person's disability is an integral part of who they are, and it becomes part of their identity; therefore, identity-first language is frequently preferred.

I am disabled.

I am autistic.

I am deaf.

Decisions, Decisions

Words are powerful. The words you choose to describe your hearing loss are important because they can convey vital information necessary for others to know what they can do to support the conversation. Please notice that I did not say "...for others to know what they can do to support you." The person with whom you're speaking needs to know what to do to support the conversation so that your communication exchange is successful. Shifting focus here from your needs to the conversation's needs empowers both people. An important part of this exercise is for you to develop words and phrases that convey your confidence to be an effective self-advocate. Conversations are between 2 or more people and everyone has an equal responsibility to understand and to be understood.

People adapt their verbal communication for others all the time, in many different situations, without even realizing it. You naturally make adjustments to your verbal communication when you speak with someone in a noisy bus versus in a quiet cafe. When you speak to a 3 year old child, you adapt your vocabulary, sentence structure and your posture to ensure they can understand you. These are not inconvenient for you to do because you know in order for this conversation to be successful, you need to make adjustments. Just as you know the child or person on the bus is not imposing an unrealistic burden on you because they need you to communicate differently than you would normally, know that the support or adaptations needed for you to understand someone communicating with you are not unreasonable.

If your hearing loss is not immediately apparent via pointing to visible hearing technology or a "Hard of Hearing" button on your chest, successfully having a conversation with a stranger in a noisy environment requires you to give them some basic information. With all the words and phrases available, a well-thought out plan ahead of time is so helpful.

Different circumstances may call for different words. What you tell the friendly barista may be different from what you say to an emergency first responder. The barista may be someone you see on a regular basis, and you enjoy the chit chat while you wait for your coffee order. Maybe it goes like this: "I am hard of hearing and I need to see your face so I can lip read. If I miss something, if you say it again a little slower, that really helps." In an emergency situation, you may have seconds to convey that you can't understand what they are saying, and maybe, "I'm deaf," is all you need to say.

Considering what people generally think when they hear words like "hard of hearing" and "deaf," can influence your decision. For some people, when they hear the term "hard of hearing" they may interpret it as "I can hear, it's just a little hard." This can cause communication difficulties if they assume you won't have a problem if they just speak up.

Using terms such as "hearing impaired" or "deaf" may convey a greater difficulty with hearing and understanding speech, and possibly the need for other accommodations. You might prefer to use "deaf" simply because it is generally understood that "deaf" conveys significant difficulty understanding speech. You might use some variation, such as "half deaf," "a little bit deaf," or "partially deaf."

Often, you will need to provide specific instructions for your communication partner. Remember, you are not burdening them, you are educating them. Sometimes, simply stating you are "hard of hearing" can be understood to mean that you can hear and understand with some "extra effort" on your part. This is a dangerous assumption, since the misconception places the burden of successful communication on you: "If you exert some extra effort, you should be able to understand me. If you don't understand, you must not be putting forth enough effort." We will go over in much more detail how to do this in chapter seven: People & Places. But for now, you will want to consider this as you make decisions about the words you use to identify your hearing loss.

MY WORDS
JOURNAL ACTIVITY

Look back at the list and words you circled on page 109. Having gone over all the terms and phrases, how do you feel about the words you have used in the past to identify your hearing loss?

_____

_____

_____

_____

_____

_____

_____

_____

_____

_____

_____

_____

_____

_____

_____

_____

_____

_____

_____

_____

_____

Based on what you've learned, what words feel the most accurate for you, for most situations (friends, family, co-workers, social gatherings)? What feels best for you, person-first or identity-first language? Are there words that might be more effective in certain situations, or with certain people, such as the emergency responder example? List them here.

_____

_____

_____

_____

_____

_____

_____

_____

_____

_____

_____

_____

_____

_____

_____

_____

_____

_____

_____

_____

Section Three

In this section, you will have lots of time to work in your journal completing activities that celebrate who you are and work to integrate your hearing loss as a part of that picture.

If you are struggling to see your hearing loss as part of your identity (still feeling denial), and if that feels like it is holding you back from self-acceptance and self-love, let's spend some time considering what your identity could be if who you are and your hearing loss were integrated.

I AM
JOURNAL ACTIVITY

To begin, use the following two pages to creatively and positively express who you are and what you love. Forget about your hearing loss right now and just spill onto the page everything that makes you feel like you. Stay positive. If negative images or words about your hearing loss emerge, let them float on by (or flip back to Processing Negative Experiences on page 71 and briefly jot them down; but return to this exercise quickly and redirect your attention to all the positive parts of you.)

Draw! List! Color! Write! Describe! What makes you YOU? What are your favorites? What are your roles in life? Who loves you? How would they describe you? No rush, take your time on this one.

If you need to see an example of a completed journal entry for this activity, see **page 124.**

I am ...

I am ...

I hope what you have recorded on these two pages is beautiful to you. You have so many amazing aspects that make you unique--thanks for taking the time to record and celebrate them.

I am ...

Katherine

Nana

Mom♡

Daughter

Partner/Wife

Sister

TRAVE

TEACHER

FRIEND

Estudiante de Español

Sewist

Neighbor

I am ...

LER

Business Owner

Author

Yogurt PLEASE!

Organizer

Designer

ADVOCATE

Fitness

Board Member

LGBTQIA+

I hope what you have recorded on these two pages is beautiful to you. You have so many amazing aspects that make you unique--thanks for taking the time to record and celebrate them.

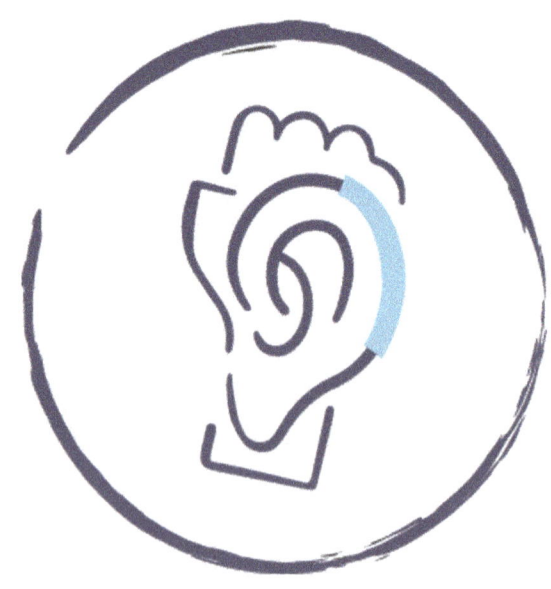

MY IDENTITY +
MY HEARING LOSS IDENTITY

Step 1: Look back at what you just created in the journal activity I am... (pages 122-123). Choose the top five things that you love. That could be any combination of colors, words, drawings, emotions, and representations that make you amazing.

Step 2: Write a brief description of each in FIVE of the circles provided on the next two pages (Leave one circle blank.)

Step 3: Add your hearing loss identity to the sixth circle. Use the words and phrases you just landed on in the My Words journal activity (pages 118-119).

Step 4: Spend some time on these pages. Color, draw, describe. Make this page as expressive and artistic as you can. Give all six parts equal attention, and feel free to overlap and merge your words and illustrations.

If you need to see an example of a completed journal entry for this activity, see page 132.

My Identity + My Hearing Loss Identity

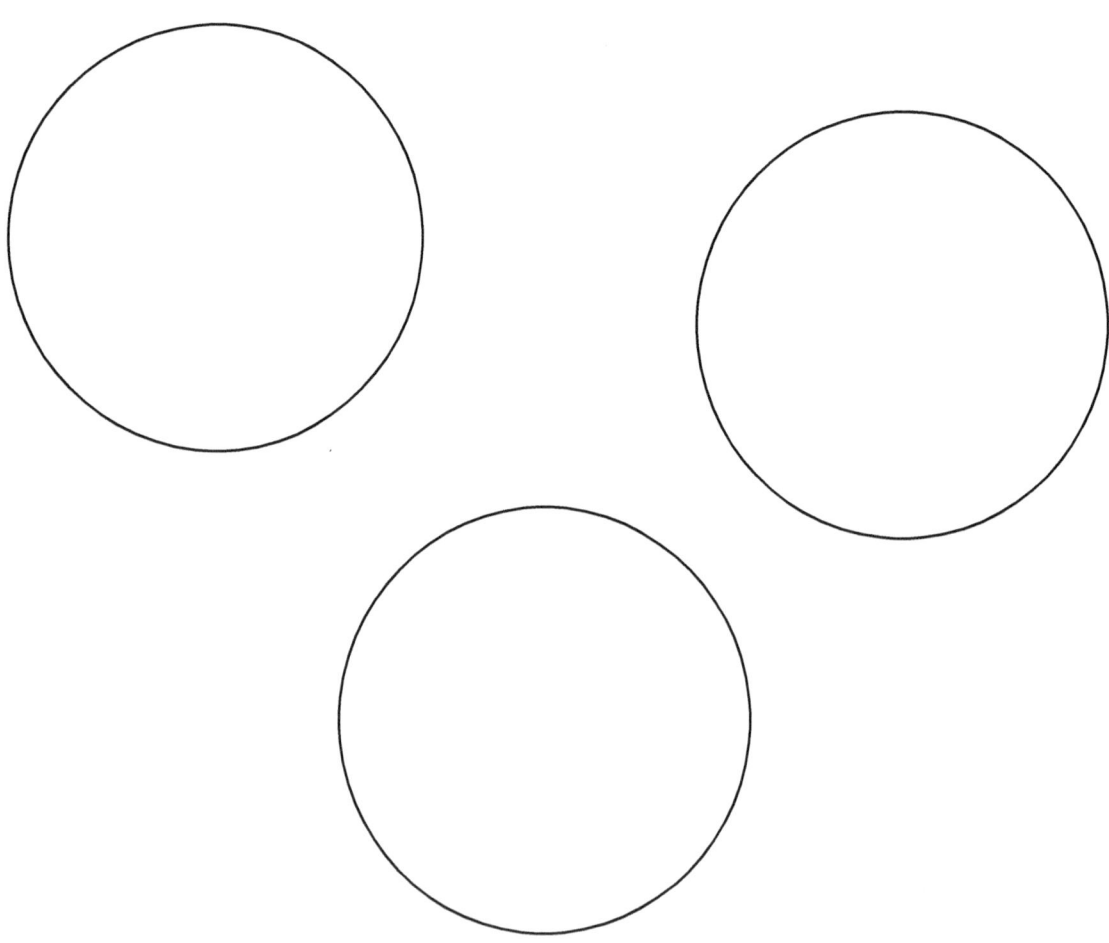

My Identity + My Hearing Loss Identity

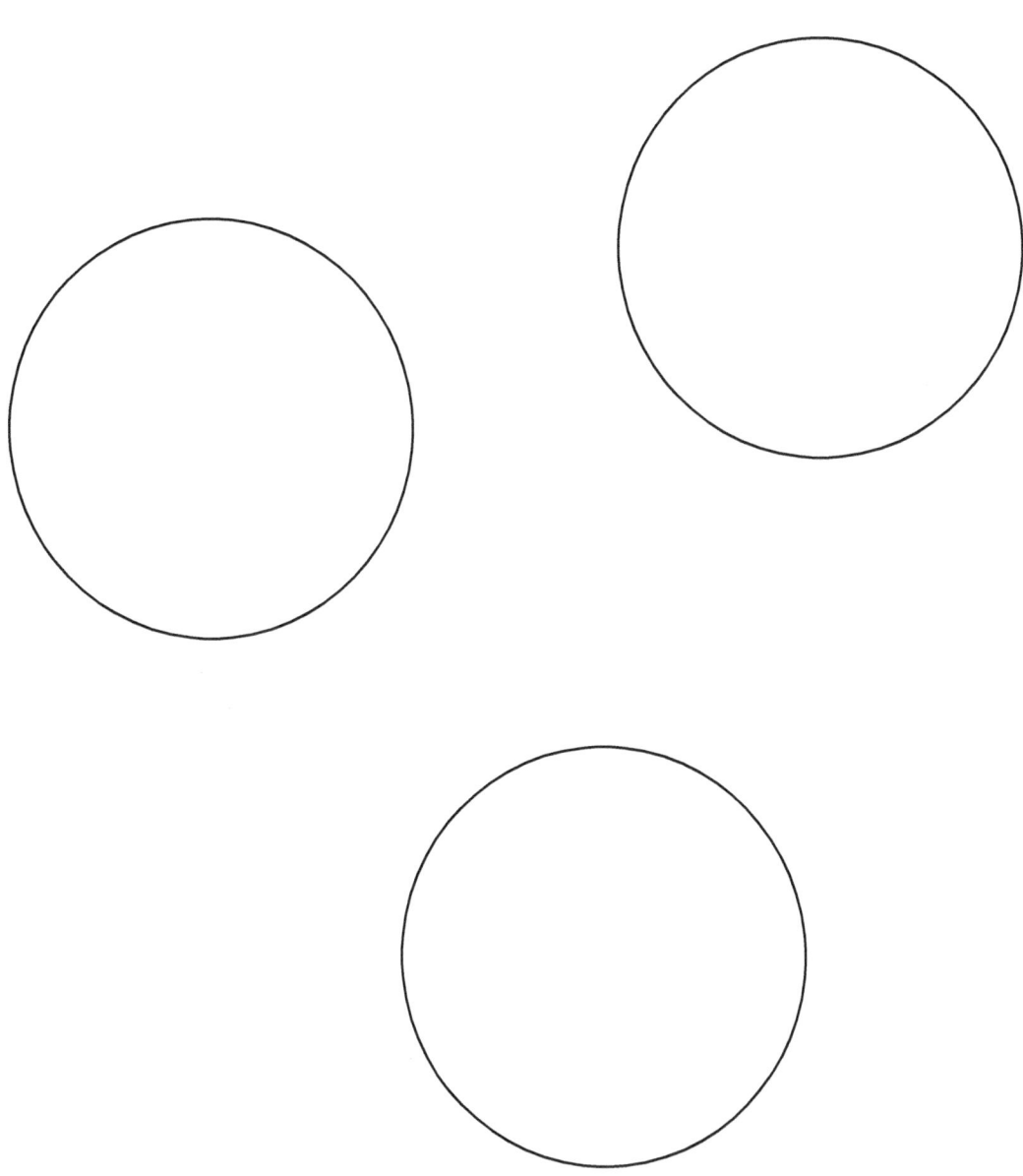

My Identity + My Hearing Loss Identity

Reflection: Finally, let's spend some time reflecting on this activity. What was it like to visually incorporate your hearing loss identity with the most important parts of who you are? Was it overwhelming? Relieving? Empowering? No big deal? Does it all fit together, or do you need some more time to embrace this piece of you?

_____

_____

_____

_____

_____

_____

_____

_____

_____

_____

_____

_____

_____

_____

_____

_____

My Identity + My Hearing Loss Identity

_____
_____
_____
_____
_____
_____
_____
_____
_____
_____
_____
_____
_____
_____
_____
_____
_____
_____
_____
_____
_____
_____
_____
_____
_____
_____

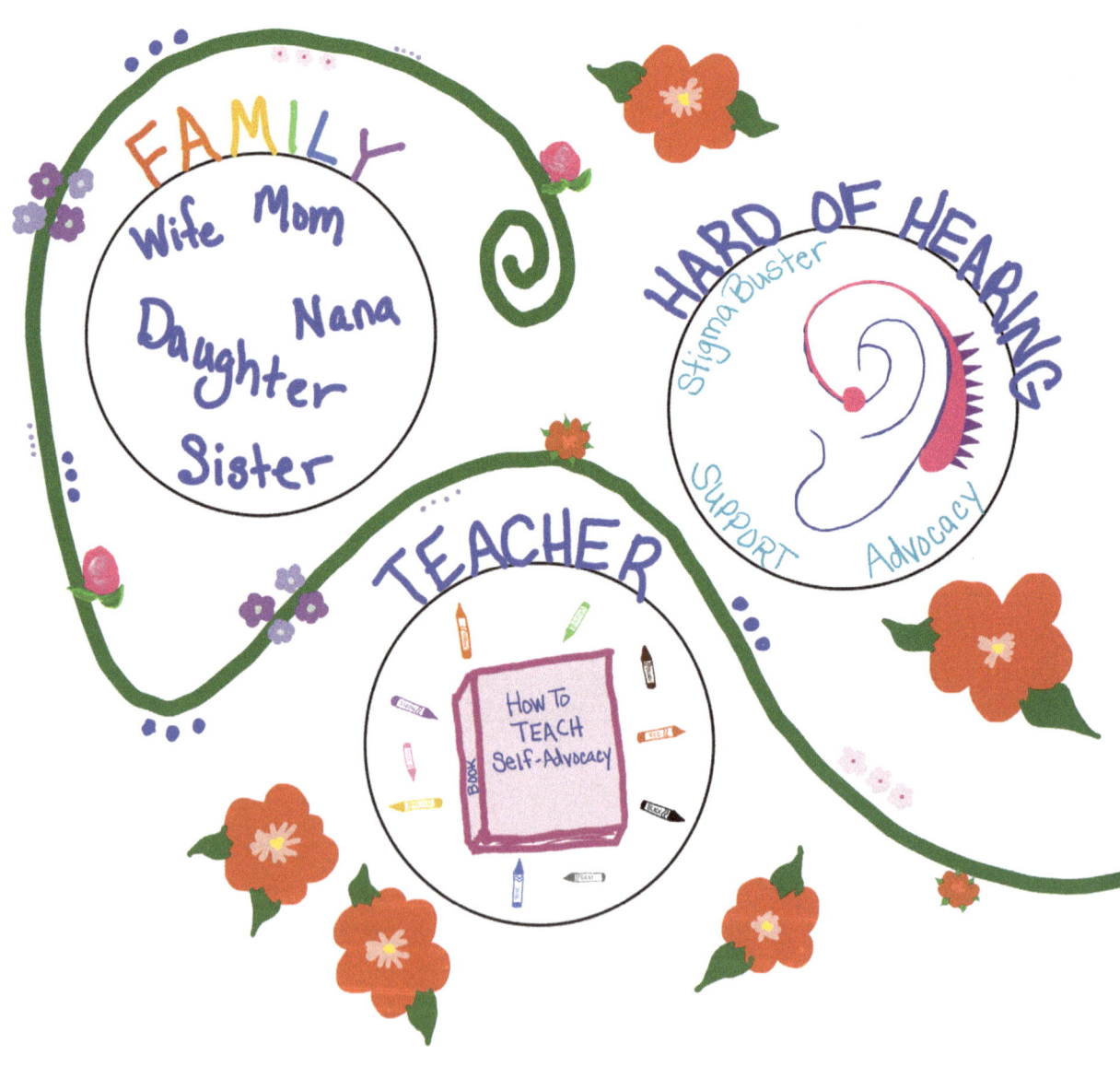

FAMILY

Wife Mom

Daughter Nana

Sister

HARD OF HEARING

Stigma Buster

Support Advocacy

TEACHER

How To TEACH Self-Advocacy

MAKER

ADVOCATE

D/HH

VOTE

LGBTQIA+

WOMEN'S RIGHTS

Access to Health Care

MENTAL HEALTH

TRAVELER

US PASSPORT

Section Four

Welcome back to chapter five: Identity & Self Love. In this section, we will focus on community and socializing.

Community

With identity comes community. Hearing loss can be isolating because it makes communication difficult. As a person with hearing loss, there are many other people out there who have struggled with the same things you do. First let's talk about the words used to define these communities.

Communities that are inclusive of all levels of hearing loss, from slight to profound, and not dependant on any one type of language (spoken vs. signed) are referred to as the d/Deaf and Hard of Hearing community, the hearing loss community, and less frequently, the deaf community (where deaf = continuum of all levels of hearing loss).

The Deaf community includes people who use sign language and participate in cultural experiences with other Deaf community members.

The Hard of Hearing community includes people who use spoken language and don't have a culture separate from the hearing world.

The hearing community is made up of people without hearing disabilities and is the dominant culture that uses spoken language. The hearing community, or the hearing world, is less educated about the unique challenges of hearing loss.

There are various organizations that serve these communities. Connecting with them can provide a real sense of belonging and offer opportunities to develop relationships with people that understand your unique experience with hearing loss. These organizations may serve on the local level, state level, nation level, or world level.

Introvert vs. Extravert

Socializing may be exhausting for you. The work you put into understanding speech, filling in missed words using context clues, and maintaining visual attention to the speaker's face is no small feat. You may feel exhausted or overwhelmed in many social settings, and this can change your behavior. Your hearing loss may push you in the direction of "introvert" or "extrovert" even if it isn't your innate personality!

Let's take a minute to consider these common personality traits, and how they might intertwine with your hearing loss.

According to Merriam-Webster, an introvert is "a typically reserved or quiet person who tends to be introspective and enjoys spending time alone," and an extrovert is "a typically gregarious and unreserved person who enjoys and seeks out social interaction."

How do you socialize? Are you the life of the party? Do you prefer to find one or two friends to chat with in a corner of the room?

You might not have realized how much your hearing loss can influence how you interact with others.

You may prefer to be a leader, gregarious and the center of attention. If you are in control of the conversation and guiding the interaction, you run a lower risk of getting lost.

You may prefer to keep your interactions intimate, chatting with one or 2 friends away from the noise of a party. These more intimate interactions give you the opportunity to control the environment, and implement strategies that make communication easier, such as asking for better lighting or noise reduction. You might be more apt to attempt to repair communication breakdowns when you miss something when you are with one or two other people versus five or six.

Are you an extrovert that longs to be more involved in the dinner party, but have resigned yourself to a more introverted set of behaviors because you've been burned too many times by your hearing loss? Do you feel stifled because you've had to curb your desire to grab the limelight?

Are you an introvert that longs to connect more deeply with one or two people at the party, but have found that it's easier to lead the conversation than it is to follow your friend's story about their trip to Asia? Do you feel robbed because you lean away from your desire to retreat to a more intimate setting?

INTROVERT VS. EXTRAVERT
JOURNAL ACTIVITY

Consider for a moment, without hearing loss, what do you truly identify with: introvert or extrovert?

_____

_____

_____

_____

_____

_____

_____

_____

_____

Using a growth mindset, what might you try in order to get back in touch with your true introverted or extroverted you?

_____

_____

_____

_____

_____

_____

_____

_____

_____

_____

_____

_____

_____

Section Five

In this final section of chapter five, you will consider how wearing hearing technology makes you feel, if you have reservations about people seeing your hearing aids or CI processors, and how to shine some positive light and energy on those limiting thoughts or feelings.

VISIBLE HEARING TECHNOLOGY & IDENTITY
JOURNAL ACTIVITY

There are many emotions and assumptions about hearing technology, mostly rooted in stigma. These preconceived ideas and gut reactions can affect your ability to accept your hearing loss and willingness to use the technology that is available.

Let's explore your current value judgments on the following pages. Allow yourself to truly respond to each image.

Visible Hearing Technology & Identity
Picture 1

Record your gut reaction to this person wearing a hearing aid by reading a word, deciding to make a mark or not, and move on. Do not judge yourself for your choices. Right now, we are exploring your preconceived ideas and unconscious thoughts about these images.

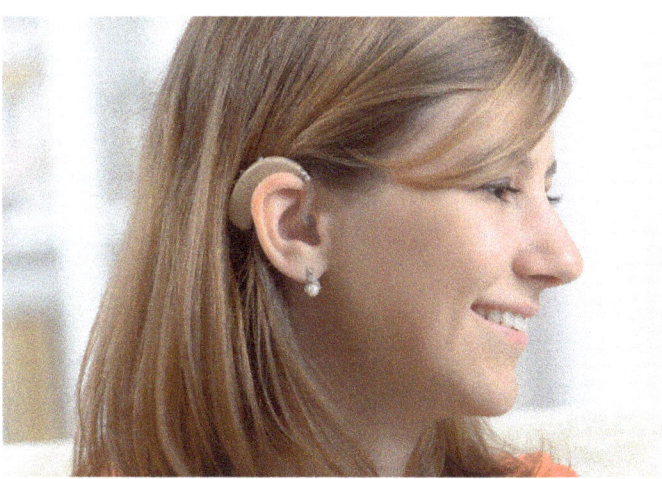

stylish	shows personality	cool
embarrassing	hide	flaunt
proud	quirky	colorful
blend in	outgoing	introvert
shy	bold	brave
humble	confident	brilliant
independent	imaginative	nondescript
passionate	social	creative
empowered	dependent	quiet
reserved	nervous	pessimistic
optimistic	discreet	boring
cheeky	unimaginative	worried
fearless	unfriendly	courageous
impartial	childish	noncommittal
ordinary	chic	serious
inspiring	no nonsense	practical
indulgent	low key	minimal

Visible Hearing Technology & Identity
Picture 2

Record your gut reaction to this person wearing glasses by reading a word, deciding to make a mark or not, and move on. Do not judge yourself for your choices. Right now, we are exploring your preconceived ideas and unconscious thoughts about these images.

stylish	shows personality	cool
embarrassing	hide	flaunt
proud	quirky	colorful
blend in	outgoing	introvert
shy	bold	brave
humble	confident	brilliant
independent	imaginative	nondescript
passionate	social	creative
empowered	dependent	quiet
reserved	nervous	pessimistic
optimistic	discreet	boring
cheeky	unimaginative	worried
fearless	unfriendly	courageous
impartial	childish	noncommittal
ordinary	chic	serious
inspiring	no nonsense	practical
indulgent	low key	minimal

Visible Hearing Technology & Identity
Picture 3

Record your gut reaction to this person wearing a decorated hearing aid by reading a word, deciding to make a mark or not, and move on. Do not judge yourself for your choices. Right now, we are exploring your preconceived ideas and unconscious thoughts about these images.

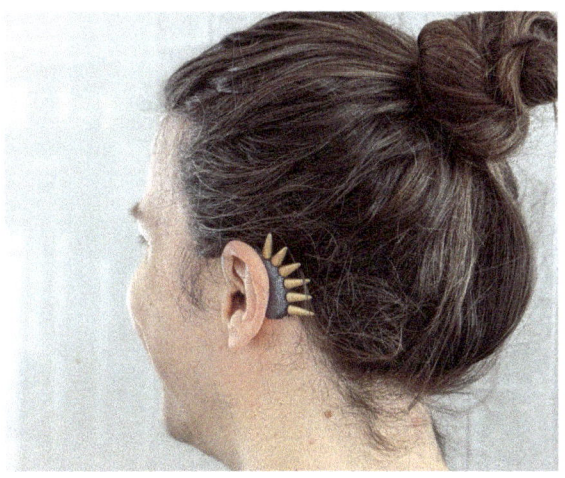

stylish	shows personality	cool
embarrassing	hide	flaunt
proud	quirky	colorful
blend in	outgoing	introvert
shy	bold	brave
humble	confident	brilliant
independent	imaginative	nondescript
passionate	social	creative
empowered	dependent	quiet
reserved	nervous	pessimistic
optimistic	discreet	boring
cheeky	unimaginative	worried
fearless	unfriendly	courageous
impartial	childish	noncommittal
ordinary	chic	serious
inspiring	no nonsense	practical
indulgent	low key	minimal

Visible Hearing Technology & Identity
Picture 4

Record your gut reaction to this person wearing bright glasses by reading a word, deciding to make a mark or not, and move on. Do not judge yourself for your choices. Right now, we are exploring your preconceived ideas and unconscious thoughts about these images.

stylish	shows personality	cool
embarrassing	hide	flaunt
proud	quirky	colorful
blend in	outgoing	introvert
shy	bold	brave
humble	confident	brilliant
independent	imaginative	nondescript
passionate	social	creative
empowered	dependent	quiet
reserved	nervous	pessimistic
optimistic	discreet	boring
cheeky	unimaginative	worried
fearless	unfriendly	courageous
impartial	childish	noncommittal
ordinary	chic	serious
inspiring	no nonsense	practical
indulgent	low key	minimal

Visible Hearing Technology & Identity
Picture 5

Record your gut reaction to this person wearing ear buds by reading a word, deciding to make a mark or not, and move on. Do not judge yourself for your choices. Right now, we are exploring your preconceived ideas and unconscious thoughts about these images.

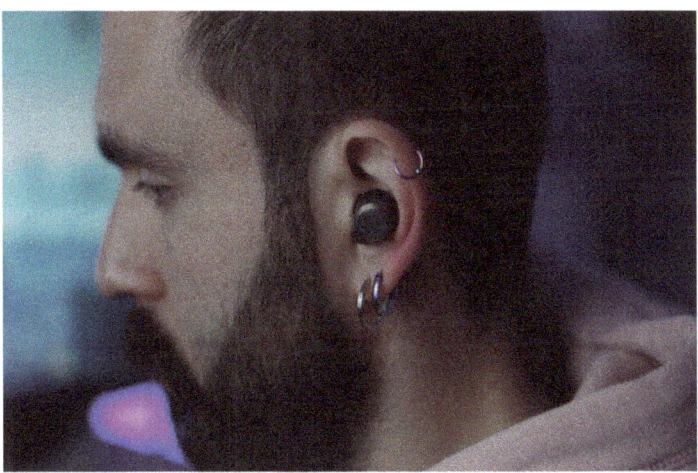

stylish	shows personality	cool
embarrassing	hide	flaunt
proud	quirky	colorful
blend in	outgoing	introvert
shy	bold	brave
humble	confident	brilliant
independent	imaginative	nondescript
passionate	social	creative
empowered	dependent	quiet
reserved	nervous	pessimistic
optimistic	discreet	boring
cheeky	unimaginative	worried
fearless	unfriendly	courageous
impartial	childish	noncommittal
ordinary	chic	serious
inspiring	no nonsense	practical
indulgent	low key	minimal

Visible Hearing Technology & Identity
Picture 6

Record your gut reaction to this person wearing sunglasses by reading a word, deciding to make a mark or not, and move on. Do not judge yourself for your choices. Right now, we are exploring your preconceived ideas and unconscious thoughts about these images.

stylish	shows personality	cool
embarrassing	hide	flaunt
proud	quirky	colorful
blend in	outgoing	introvert
shy	bold	brave
humble	confident	brilliant
independent	imaginative	nondescript
passionate	social	creative
empowered	dependent	quiet
reserved	nervous	pessimistic
optimistic	discreet	boring
cheeky	unimaginative	worried
fearless	unfriendly	courageous
impartial	childish	noncommittal
ordinary	chic	serious
inspiring	no nonsense	practical
indulgent	low key	minimal

Visible Hearing Technology & Identity

Reflection: Look back at your reactions to the images. What do you notice? Were your overall feelings about the images representing hearing technology (image 1 and 3) negative or positive? Do you wish you felt differently about your reaction to any of the images? Why?

_____
_____
_____
_____
_____
_____
_____
_____
_____
_____
_____
_____
_____
_____
_____
_____
_____
_____
_____
_____

The Stigma of Hearing Technology

Your preconceived ideas about hearing technology have been developed over time. Think about the messages you've received about hearing technology over your lifetime. Hearing devices carry a stigma in a way that glasses do not. Companies advertise their hearing aids as "invisible" or "barely noticeable." Hearing aids and cochlear implant processors come in colors meant to blend in with hair or skin (although this is slowly changing). You may not have even been asked what color you would prefer. Yet when purchasing glasses, people are given a wide array of styles, colors and shapes, and encouraged to show off their personalities through their design choices.

Maybe you feel a hearing aid or cochlear implant processor makes you appear old, or incompetent, or weird. Maybe it's just always been a part of you, and you don't really think much about it. You may feel shame or embarrassment if your hearing technology is revealed or talked about. You might be ambivalent, or even proud of your hearing technology. Maybe you love your hearing technology, bling it out, and don't care who sees it. Perhaps you prefer people to notice your hearing technology because it reduces the need to disclose your hearing loss—it does the talking for you.

HEARING TECHNOLOGY IN A POSITIVE LIGHT
JOURNAL ACTIVITY

If you had some negative reactions to the images about hearing technology, let's explore how you might reframe those feelings. If you could block out those preconceived notions and the opinions of others, what words might you choose to describe your hearing technology in a positive light?

stylish	shows personality	cool
embarrassing	hide	flaunt
proud	quirky	colorful
blend in	outgoing	introvert
shy	bold	brave
humble	confident	brilliant
independent	imaginative	nondescript
passionate	social	creative
empowered	dependent	quiet
reserved	nervous	pessimistic
optimistic	discreet	boring
cheeky	unimaginative	worried
fearless	unfriendly	courageous
impartial	childish	noncommittal
ordinary	chic	serious
inspiring	no nonsense	practical
indulgent	low key	minimal

Hearing Technology in a Positive Light

What would your hearing technology look like if it could reflect your word choices? Draw your device(s) and add color to match your word choices!

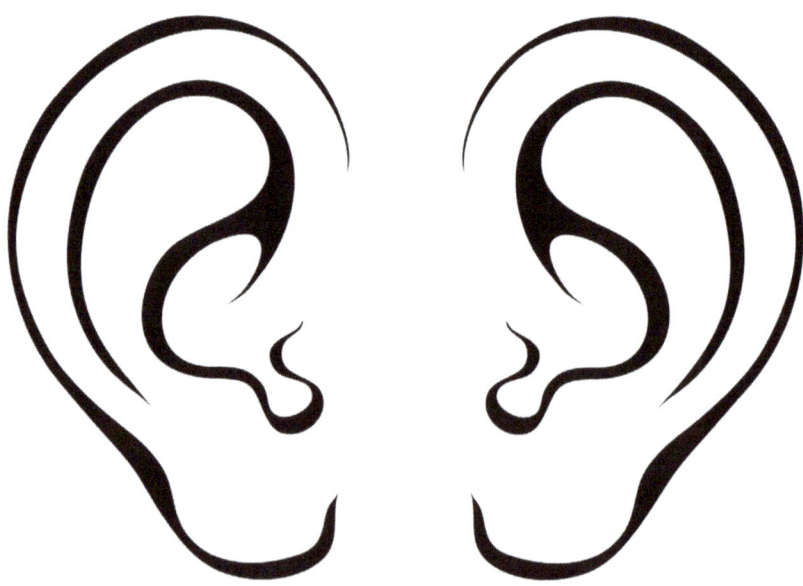

6 | technology & accommodations

Section One

Welcome to chapter six: Technology & Accommodations. In this section, we'll go over the goals for this chapter, and begin our deep dive into the process of obtaining personal hearing technology: hearing aids and cochlear implant processors, and their accessories.

Chapter 6 Goals:

- I can find a qualified audiologist in my area.
- I am well-informed about the different types of personal hearing technology and accessories available.
- I know how to find detailed information about personal hearing technology and use that information at my audiology appointment.
- I give my audiologist detailed feedback about my personal hearing technology and advocate for improvements in programming and options.
- I am well-informed about assistive technology and accommodations that are available to the d/Deaf and Hard of Hearing community, and I know how to access them.

Introduction–Personal Hearing Technology

Whether you are just now considering hearing aids and/or cochlear implants, or you have worn them for years, it is important to be informed when it comes to choosing the right technology for you. In this chapter, we will touch briefly on the basics, but our main focus will be how to become an active, empowered self-advocate who digs deeper into the process than simply choosing from the 1 or 2 options recommended by your audiologist. Now, don't get me wrong. Your audiologist is the expert in hearing technology, but doing a little research and preparation before your appointment can empower you to ask more questions and ensure your needs are fully taken into consideration when choosing the best devices for you.

Step One: Find Your Professional

Hands down, most experienced hearing aid users will recommend you find an audiologist (Doctor of Audiology–AuD) rather than a hearing care specialist or hearing aid fitting specialist. Audiologists have significantly more expertise, come from accredited educational institutions, and can provide much more value in exchange for your time and money.

Time is a key factor in this process. Purchasing and being fit with new hearing aids or cochlear implant processors is not usually a one or two appointment matter. When you purchase your devices, a large portion of that purchase price may be prepaid support and tweaking. Plan to see your audiologist as many times as needed to get your devices optimally tuned to your key listening environments.

Many audiologists only fit certain brands of devices. If you have your eye on a specific hearing aid from a specific manufacturer, you will want to find out ahead of time if it will be available at your chosen audiologist's office.

If you need help finding a good audiologist, check with local organizations and agencies to get recommendations.

Check out hearingoutloud.net tips on how to find an audiologist in your area.

QUESTIONS FOR
POTENTIAL AUDIOLOGISTS
JOURNAL ACTIVITY

Complete this activity if you are currently looking for an audiologist. If not, you may need it in the future. Use this question guide to make an informed decision on which audiologist is the best fit for you. Jot down the name and contact information for each at the top of the chart.

	Option 1 Name: Contact:	Option 2 Name: Contact:	Option 3 Name: Contact:
Are you a licensed doctor of audiology?			
Do you take my insurance?			
What brands of hearing instruments do you offer?			
Do you offer accessories or other assistive listening devices?			
Are follow up appointments for adjustments or questions covered in the purchase price?			
What's your trial period policy?			
What's your return policy?			
What support do you provide during and after the trial?			

Section Two

In this section, you will learn how to do important research before your audiology appointment.

Step Two: Do Your Homework

Once you've found an audiologist and have scheduled an appointment, it's time to research. If you are considering hearing aids or cochlear implants for the very first time, or if you are an experienced user looking for replacement or upgraded devices, the entire process can feel a bit overwhelming, but I strongly suggest you dedicate time to familiarize yourself with the different devices available, and learn about the multitude of features.

From my personal experiences as a consumer, as a teacher for students who are deaf and hard of hearing, and as a friend advising others who are new to hearing loss, audiologists have a finite amount of time to spend with you. They want you to experience the maximum benefit of the devices you purchase. For new users, they recognize the amount of information can be overwhelming, and they want to simplify the experience as much as possible. If you are new to hearing loss, and new to wearing hearing aids, all of this can leave your head spinning.

Only you can know what you really need in a hearing device. Your audiologist will spend time asking you about the different environments in which you struggle to hear and understand, but they will likely not have time to really discuss these in depth. Audiologists are looking to maximize the benefits of your short appointments. Learning how to care for your hearing aids, change batteries, switch programs, and more, takes time and an adjustment period. This is why, based on your hearing test and a brief interview, audiologists will often recommend one or two options they feel will give you the best chance at becoming a successful hearing device user. If you haven't researched brands and features of the models suggested, you may miss opportunities to find the best devices for your lifestyle.

Power Options

Most hearing aids and cochlear implant processors come with a variety of power options, including rechargeable lithium-ion batteries and disposable zinc-air batteries.

Rechargeable options are convenient if you are conscientious about sticking to a routine of placing your devices on the charger each night. They generally last 12+ hours even with bluetooth streaming. Rechargeable batteries allow you to go about your day without low battery warnings and changing the batteries in the middle of your day. Generally, rechargeable options require a slightly larger sized device. The drawback to rechargeable devices is that you will need to remove them to charge if they run out of power before you do, and if there are issues with the batteries charging correctly, your audiologist may need to send your hearing aids to the manufacturer for replacement batteries, leaving you without hearing aids for a week or more.

Disposable batteries offer an immediate remedy if you run out of power–simply change them and you're good to go. This option does come with additional cost as you will need to purchase a supply of batteries on an ongoing basis. Disposable batteries also come in various sizes allowing for smaller hearing devices.

Brands

There are about six major brands of hearing aids in North America: Sonova (which includes Phonak and Unitron), ReSound, Siemens (which includes Signia and Rexton,) Starkey, Widex, and Oticon. There are 3 cochlear implant manufacturers: (Cochlear, Med-El, and Advanced Bionics.) These companies offer a range of different devices in a variety of styles. Cochlear implant users stick with the brand with which you were implanted, but there is new innovation in the style and features of processors. Hearing aid users have greater flexibility between brands; however, it is important to remember not all audiologists carry all brands of hearing aids. If you have your eye on a certain brand or model of hearing aid, check with the audiologist to find out if they provide that brand.

Most brands carry accessories as well, which we will go over in more detail in the next few sections. If there is an accessory you would like to use, check the brand and consider asking for that brand of hearing aid as well. An example of this is the Roger microphones by Phonak. This is an entire line of remote (not attached to your ear) microphones that integrate with your hearing aids or cochlear implants and can greatly improve speech understanding in noise and at a distance. While these microphones can be used with hearing aids and cochlear implants not manufactured by Phonak, the digital connection is seamless with the Phonak hearing aids that allow the receivers to be programmed into the hearing aids themselves, eliminating the need for attachments clipped onto your devices.

 Check out hearingoutloud.net for links to suppliers of hearing aids and cochlear implants.

Styles, Features & Performance Levels

Hearing aids and cochlear implants come in a number of different styles. Depending on how you feel about wearing visible hearing technology, I do encourage you not to let "invisibility" be the number one determining factor for choosing your hearing devices. While empowered self-advocates inform people about their hearing loss, sometimes visible devices may actually be desired to avoid the constant need to self-disclose. Also, it's important to know when considering one style of hearing aid versus another, there may be important feature trade-offs if small and discrete is a big focus for you. Ideally, you want to hear and understand better in many environments, and when this is your primary objective without concern for size and shape, you may be delighted with the results. Certainly, if you would be more comfortable with something less obvious, there is no judgment! The important thing is you find something you love and something you will wear. It does no good sitting in the box.

Hearing aids come with various features, such as special programming, rechargeable batteries, Bluetooth streaming, remote control apps, and other functions. Devices are also usually offered at different performance levels (corresponding with different price points.) The performance levels may range from basic to premium, and as you move up from basic, more features are offered, with the premium performance level offering all the features available for that particular model. This allows audiologists to offer good hearing aids at more affordable prices, and premium hearing aids with enhanced features for specialized needs.

When you do your research, look at the major brand websites and view the variety of shapes and sizes of hearing devices. The particular features of a hearing aid are often offered in different styles, such as behind the ear and in the ear models. Pay attention to the way the devices are named.

Using Phonak as an example, they offer the Audéo Paradise and the Virto Paradise. The Audéo Paradise model is a receiver in the canal, or RIC, hearing aid and the Virto Paradise is an in the ear, ITE, hearing aid. Both use Phonak's Paradise platform for sound processing technology.

It is important to know the various features and performance levels offered for the different hearing aids. This is sometimes difficult to find, but you can search online, or ask the audiologist to show you the list of features and performance levels available.

Back to our example with the 2 Phonak Paradise hearing aids, the Audéo RIC model has a tap feature that allows you to tap the ear to turn on and off bluetooth streaming. The Virto does not offer this feature. The premium performance level (90) for Paradise platform hearing aids includes "speech in loud noise," "speech in car," and "comfort in echo." These are not included in the "advanced (70)," "standard (60)," and "essential (50)" performance levels. If these are critical listening situations for you, it's important your audiologist knows.

How can you find the features list for a hearing aid or CI processor? Researching major brand websites will help you become familiar with the styles, platforms and features available. Don't be afraid to click around and explore on these websites. On many of the major brand websites, the "For Professionals" link provides more specific information about the devices. Most brands offer side by side comparisons of the devices and performance levels available.

T-Coil or Telecoil

The telecoil (often called a t-coil) permits coupling of a personal hearing aid to sources of electromagnetic energy, such as a hearing aid compatible telephone or an induction loop. Many hearing aids come with a telecoil, but you may need to specifically request this feature from your audiologist to ensure it is included in the devices you purchase. Loops are often installed in public places such as churches, meeting halls, and live performance theaters. See "Induction Loops" in the Accommodations and Assistive Technology portion of this chapter for more information (page 174).

Auracast

Auracast is a brand new technology designed to improve audio accessibility for not only those of us with hearing loss, but for other disabilities and the general population. It uses advanced broadcasting methods to deliver high-quality audio directly to hearing aids, cochlear implants, earbuds, and headphones via Bluetooth.

Auracast is different from the Bluetooth we have used in recent years because it allows audio to be broadcasted from various sources, such as public address systems or personal devices, to multiple receivers simultaneously. Public vendors will be able to broadcast their audio to many users, and you will have the ability to receive the signal based on which channel you choose. The process will be very similar to choosing a WiFi source from a menu of local options. Vendors will be able to broadcast multiple streams of audio, including information in various different languages, or provide audio descriptions of visual information for the blind and visually impaired. Imagine the benefits of being able to directly connect with the audio system at an airport gate or train station! Receive clear audio streamed through your hearing aids or cochlear implants while watching a movie or theater production! Tune in to a lecture from your seat without needing to give the instructor a separate remote microphone! Get your fitness instructor's voice directly streamed so you can hear every word! Auracast will also become available on your personal devices, so you can stream audio from your computer, smartphone, and televisions directly to your ears, and you can share that music or movie with friends and family if they have Auracast receivers as well.

Perhaps one of the most exciting aspects of Auracast is that it will have wide appeal to the general population, driving the need for public venues and all personal devices to adopt this new technology. It is important to know, however, that your hearing aid or cochlear implant will only be able to connect if the device is "Auracast ready," meaning it must include a special receiver in order for you to make the connection. Many hearing aid and cochlear implant manufacturers at the time of publication (Fall 2024) do not yet sell hearing aids that are Auracast ready. You definitely want to have a conversation with your audiologist if you are considering new devices to find out if Auracast will be an option in your new aids.

Not a Perfect Fix

Hearing aids and cochlear implant processors can help you hear better than you can without them, but they have their limitations. They can not replace or replicate natural hearing. Even with amazing technological advances, you will still have difficulty hearing and understanding speech, especially in noise. This is especially hard for hearing people to understand. There is a common misconception that hearing aids can do for the ears what glasses can do for the eyes. Glasses and contact lenses can actually correct many vision impairments, making text and images go from blurred to crystal clear. They can also correct vision close up and at a distance. This is just not true with hearing aids and cochlear implants. Accessories can help.

Section Three

In this section, we continue step two: Do Your Homework. Next you will learn about the different types of accessories frequently available for hearing aids and CI processors, take a few moments to consider the cost of personal hearing technology devices, and discuss the journal activity "Preparing for My Audiology Appt."

Accessories

There are many accessories available today that can enhance the function of your hearing aids or cochlear implant processors.

Remote Control

The ability to control your hearing devices remotely, either using a handheld remote or an app on your phone has the benefits of easily making program or volume changes to your devices without fiddling with the tiny buttons on your hearing aids or processors. These adjustments may change the direction of your hearing aid microphones, focusing on the person talking in front of you instead of the noise behind you, or allow you to change the volume on one or both ears.

Remote Microphones

Your hearing devices are probably equipped with multiple microphones at your ear level. With newer technology, the programming of your devices may automatically turn on and off different microphones depending on what you are listening to. There are limitations to these microphones though. They really only do their best work when the sound source is close to you without a lot of extra noise. When you are trying to listen to a person giving a presentation 15 feet away from you, or straining to hear your partner talking in a noisy restaurant, your hearing devices may not perform well enough for you to enjoy these experiences.

Remote microphones are small devices that can be clipped on a shirt or lain flat on a table. They direct the sound right to your ear(s) as if you were sitting right next to the person speaking. These microphones can prioritize the voices it picks up over the voices and sounds happening around you. Some microphones can also perform in "interview mode" which allows you to point the microphone at a 45° angle, picking up the voice of someone talking about 10 feet away.

There are usually two levels of remote microphones: those that use a digital (DM) or FM signal, such as Phonak's Roger microphones, and those that operate via bluetooth, often called mini-mic, partner mic, or multi-mic. The DM/FM mics are generally more expensive but may have higher quality sound or stronger connectivity.

This new technology can be a game changer for you. They can allow you to enjoy environments like sporting events and restaurants that you might be avoiding. When it is clipped on a person's shirt, you can hear them clearly in the car, walking, biking and shopping. If you've struggled with these kinds of situations, I highly recommend exploring the use of a remote microphone.

TV Connector

Many hearing aid and cochlear implant manufacturers offer TV connectors which will stream the television sound wirelessly directly to your hearing devices.

Streamers

Using bluetooth technology, streamers are small devices that are worn clipped to your shirt or on a lanyard around your neck. These allow you to stream via bluetooth from your phone, laptop or tablet to your hearing devices. However, there are more and more models of hearing aids and sound processors that are bluetooth capable that don't require a streamer.

A Word About Cost

Hearing technology is expensive. Many health insurance companies do not cover them for adults. The decision to purchase hearing technology is a major one, but if it is possible for you, I encourage you to pursue this option. If you do not use sign language, hearing and speaking are what connects you to others—the people you love, the people you work with, and the people in your community. Hearing better may allow you to enjoy television shows, an elementary school play, podcasts, movies, audiobooks, and your favorite music. If these are things you've been missing, consider the cost in lost quality of life versus the cost of hearing technology.

Most of the time, the price of hearing aids includes a lot more than just the hearing aids. Sold as a bundle, the cost usually includes the hearing test, consultation, initial fitting, and all follow-up adjustments, routine cleanings and a warranty that can range from one to three years. These services alone, priced separately, would likely add into the thousands of dollars.

There are funding options to help you obtain hearing aids and accessories. If you need these devices in order to obtain a college education or to do your job, your state's Division of Vocational Rehabilitation can often provide help. Other agencies and programs can also provide help to fund your hearing devices.

 Check out hearingoutloud.net for links to major agencies and resources.

Whenever I consider a big purchase, I try to weigh what amount of value the purchase will add to my life. Smartphones and laptops are a good example. How frequently do we use our phones and computers, and for what tasks? They have become multi-use necessities for most of us. Purchasing a new phone for $800 that I will use multiple (let's say 10) times per day every day for two years will cost me a little over $0.10 per day, not including the cost of the data plan.

Let's say purchasing two new high performance bluetooth hearing aids, a remote DM microphone, hearing test, consultation, follow up adjustments, cleanings and warranty cost about $8000. If the average lifespan of hearing aids is about seven years, and I wear them 12 hours per day, that's about $0.27 an hour, or $3.24 per day. To me, that's the cost of a coffee, and the improvement in quality of life for that cost is reasonable to me.

In another example, let's consider two new mid-level performance hearing aids with a partner mic. Including the costs of the professional and warranty, this may cost about $6,000. The daily cost for seven years and 12 hours wear per day is about $0.20 per hour, or $2.34 per day.

Keep in mind, there is little cost to a trial (more about that in a moment). If you haven't tried hearing devices before, I encourage you to give them an honest try.

There is only limited time an audiologist can spend getting to know you and your needs. Prior to your appointment, decide what is important to you. Providing this information to your audiologist will help them offer devices that will best meet your needs.

PREPARING FOR YOUR
AUDIOLOGY APPOINTMENT
JOURNAL ACTIVITY

How are you feeling about this appointment? Is this the first time you will have had your hearing tested? Are you prepared for a new or changed diagnosis? Do you expect to find out your hearing may be better or worse?

_____

_____

_____

_____

_____

_____

_____

_____

Are you prepared to consider the cost of new devices? Do you have a limit you can spend? If you have health insurance, do you know if hearing aids/cochlear implant processors are covered? Do you need financial assistance?

_____

_____

_____

_____

_____

_____

_____

_____

Preparing for Your Audiology Appointment

List your medications:	
Brief health history:	
Brief work history:	
List exposure to loud noise:	
When did you notice a change in your hearing?	
How do you feel your hearing has changed?	
Which situations and settings are the most difficult for you?	
What do you need your hearing devices to help you with the most?	

Preparing for Your Audiology Appointment

IMPORTANT	VERY IMPORTANT	
[]	[]	Style: _____
[]	[]	Color: _____
[]	[]	Programmable
[]	[]	Rechargable
[]	[]	Bluetooth streaming or wireless connectivity
[]	[]	Remote control app
[]	[]	Telecoil
[]	[]	Auracast
[]	[]	Directional microphones
[]	[]	Background noise suppression
[]	[]	Feedback suppression
[]	[]	Wind noise suppression
[]	[]	Comfort in reverberating spaces (echo)
[]	[]	Music program
[]	[]	Tinnitus management
[]	[]	Accessory–Remote control
[]	[]	Accessory–Remote microphone
[]	[]	Accessory–Multimodal DM microphone (i.e. Phonak Roger On)
[]	[]	Accessory–TV connector
[]	[]	Accessory–Connectivity for landline or office phone
[]	[]	Other: _____
[]	[]	Other: _____

Section Four

In this section, you will learn about the very important Step Three: Feedback and Follow-Up, and we will go over the journal activity "Feedback and Follow-Up Diary."

Step Three: Feedback & Follow-Up

When you receive new devices, you usually have a trial period which allows you to use the devices for a set amount of time (often 30 days) with a money back guarantee, sometimes minus a relatively small fee. This time is crucial for you to get the most out of your investment.

Wear the new devices with regularity. If you have never worn hearing aids before, your brain needs time to recalibrate and adjust to hearing sounds you haven't heard in quite some time. Wearing your hearing aids for 10-12 hours per day, seven days a week will give you the best chances of becoming accustomed to them, and ample opportunity to judge their effectiveness in a variety of listening situations.

Hearing aids are computer programmable devices. Before your first fitting, the audiologist sets them with their best guess for good sound quality in a variety of listening situations. However, these settings can always be tweaked based on your feedback. I encourage you to be picky. Keep good records. Give your audiologist lots of feedback. In which situations do you notice an improvement compared to your previous devices or when you had no devices at all? Which situations are still difficult? How is the sound quality when using different program options? If you're streaming music or phone calls, how does it sound? What would you change? If you're unhappy with certain settings or listening environments, there are a multitude of adjustments that can be made. Follow up with as many appointments as you need to get the settings just right.

FEEDBACK AND FOLLOW-UP DIARY
JOURNAL ACTIVITY

This is a 21-day feedback and follow-up diary for you to record your experiences during a hearing device trial period. This feedback will be extremely helpful when you see the audiologist to discuss issues and programming changes.

Date	Wearing hours		DAY ONE
Listening situations	Positives	Negatives	
Questions			

Date	Wearing hours		DAY TWO
Listening situations	Positives	Negatives	
Questions			

Date	Wearing hours		DAY THREE
Listening situations	Positives	Negatives	
Questions			

Feedback and Follow-Up Diary

DAY FOUR

Date	Wearing hours	
Listening situations	Positives	Negatives
Questions		

DAY FIVE

Date	Wearing hours	
Listening situations	Positives	Negatives
Questions		

DAY SIX

Date	Wearing hours	
Listening situations	Positives	Negatives
Questions		

Feedback and Follow-Up Diary

Date	Wearing hours		DAY SEVEN
Listening situations	Positives	Negatives	
Questions			

Date	Wearing hours		DAY EIGHT
Listening situations	Positives	Negatives	
Questions			

Date	Wearing hours		DAY NINE
Listening situations	Positives	Negatives	
Questions			

Feedback and Follow-Up Diary

DAY TEN

Date	Wearing hours	
Listening situations	Positives	Negatives
Questions		

DAY ELEVEN

Date	Wearing hours	
Listening situations	Positives	Negatives
Questions		

DAY TWELVE

Date	Wearing hours	
Listening situations	Positives	Negatives
Questions		

Feedback and Follow-Up Diary

Date	Wearing hours		**DAY THIRTEEN**
Listening situations	Positives	Negatives	
Questions			

Date	Wearing hours		**DAY FOURTEEN**
Listening situations	Positives	Negatives	
Questions			

Date	Wearing hours		**DAY FIFTEEN**
Listening situations	Positives	Negatives	
Questions			

Feedback and Follow-Up Diary

DAY SIXTEEN

Date	Wearing hours	
Listening situations	Positives	Negatives
Questions		

DAY SEVENTEEN

Date	Wearing hours	
Listening situations	Positives	Negatives
Questions		

DAY EIGHTEEN

Date	Wearing hours	
Listening situations	Positives	Negatives
Questions		

Feedback and Follow-Up Diary

Date	Wearing hours		DAY NINTEEN
Listening situations	Positives	Negatives	
Questions			

Date	Wearing hours		DAY TWENTY
Listening situations	Positives	Negatives	
Questions			

Date	Wearing hours		DAY TWENTY-ONE
Listening situations	Positives	Negatives	
Questions			

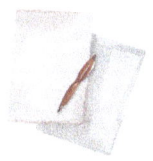

Section Five

In this section you will learn about the many different types of accommodations and assistive technology.

Accommodations and Assistive Technology

In addition to personal hearing technology such as hearing aids and cochlear implants, there are a wide variety of accommodations and other assistive technology devices that can help you in your day to day life.

Captioning

Captions are running text that displays spoken words in visual form.

Closed captioning is text that is displayed only when the feature is turned on, or when using a special device to view them. They are closed to the general viewing audience, but visible when activated or using individual viewing devices.

Open captioning is text that is displayed on the screen for the general viewing audience. Sometimes it is "burned" into the original video, or in the case of a movie theater, the captions are displayed directly on the screen for every movie goer to see.

Automated captions, or computer generated captions, are captions that use voice recognition technology to translate the spoken word to text. While not 100% accurate, this technology has come a long way and can sometimes be a great option in a pinch.

Live captions, or real-time captioning, sometimes referred to as CART (Communication Access Realtime Translation), are captions that are provided using a human to translate spoken word to text. These are the most accurate and reliable form of captions for in-person and virtual meetings. In order to be ADA-compliant, live captioning is required versus computer generated captions. This doesn't require the person to physically be in the room. They can be virtual if the situation provides high quality audio to the transcriptionist. In some situations, you can request the transcript for your reference instead of taking notes. This is not always allowed, so be sure to ask ahead of time.

Television: You may already use captions when you watch television. If you don't, I encourage you to try them. You can usually turn them on in the settings section of your tv. The option may be under the "Accessibility" or "Audio" or "Display" menu options. You can also change the caption display settings, including color and size. It takes a little time to get used to them, but once you try them, you may be surprised how much more you enjoy watching your favorite shows.

Movie theaters: Most movie theaters offer captioning devices that you use right at your seat. Sometimes they attach in the drink cup holder, and newer versions are displayed using special glasses. Not all movies provide a captioning file, so not all movies will not have this option. It's always good to check ahead of time. If you've never used them before, you usually need to request them at the ticket counter.

Live performances: Many live performances, such as Broadway plays, have real-time captioning available. Ask when you are purchasing your tickets.

Work or school: If you require captions in order to fully access auditory information at school or at work, real-time captioning is an accommodation you may have a right to under the Americans with Disabilities Act. The process to request them may depend on your particular situation. In a university, find the office that provides support to students with disabilities and make a request through them. At work, contact your HR department or speak directly with your supervisor. In chapter seven: People and Places, we will go over how to confidently have these conversations.

Speaking on the phone: There are two options for captions while speaking on the phone. You can try apps or accessibility settings in your smartphone that will provide computer-generated captions.

Another option using any kind of phone (landline, business phone, cell phone, smartphone) is using a free live captioning service with a live person providing transcription of the phone conversation. These services are provided free because they are certified by the FCC (Federal Communications Commission) and receive funding from the TRS (Telecommunications Relay Service) fund. There are also landline phones with captioning screens built in for use with real-time caption services. There is often funding available if you need equipment for telecommunications. Check with your local disability resource office.

Home and other social settings: If you have a smartphone or tablet, an automated captioning app can provide captions for you anywhere. As long as you have decent sound quality, flip on the captioning app and hold it next to the person talking. You might be surprised how accurate it can be.

 Check out hearingoutloud.net for captioning resources.

Assistive Listening Devices and FM/DM Systems

FM listening systems, and the newer DM listening systems, can work in conjunction with hearing aids and cochlear implants (see features and accessories in the previous section of this chapter: Personal Hearing Technology). These systems can also work with stand alone receivers, such as headphones or earpieces provided at the venue. They are generally available at movie theaters, live performance venues, and churches and are located at the ticket or other information desks.

Induction Loops

In some public places, such as churches, meeting halls and live performance theaters, induction loops are installed to send the audio signal from the venue's sound system directly to hearing aids using their t-coil, or telecoil, setting. This can enhance your ability to hear and understand what is being said. Not all hearing aids are equipped with t-coils, so this may be something to add to your list when seeing an audiologist for new devices. The telecoil permits coupling of the personal hearing aid to sources of electromagnetic energy, such as a hearing aid compatible telephone or an induction loop. The induction loop provides a magnetic, wireless signal that is picked up by hearing devices with telecoils. When hearing aid users are inside the loop and their t-coil setting is activated, any conversation being broadcast on the facility's audio system — ie, a church sermon or stage performance — is sent directly to the telecoil in their hearing device. This feature not only extends the listening range of hearing devices, it also eliminates unwanted background noise, to increase listening comprehension and enjoyment. Ask at the information desk or look for this symbol to find out if a hearing loop is installed.

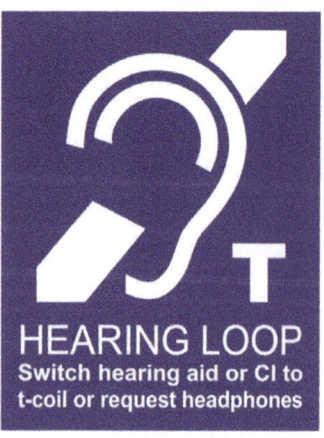

Seating

Preferential seating can provide better access simply by moving the location of your seat. In a lecture or presentation setting, most people with hearing loss prefer to sit toward the front, but not the very front row. This allows better visual access to the speaker's face and reduces the distance sound must travel to reach your ears. Sitting in the second or third row provides visual access to your peers, where you can pick up on visual cues of directions you may have missed. If they are all getting out their notebooks or turning the page in a book, you can follow along better than if you were sitting in the very front row.

In a small group situation, you might ask for your group to move to a quieter location, or for everyone to sit in a circle so you can easily see who is speaking and benefit from lip reading.

If you have unilateral hearing loss (hearing loss in one ear) or better hearing in one ear than the other, changing seating to favor the better side is always helpful. Consider this as well when you choose your seat in a lecture hall–sit in the front second or third row with your better ear toward the speaker.

Choosing your seat location in a noisy environment, such as a restaurant, requires a lot of forethought. Tables closer to the bar or the kitchen will have more background noise. Look for speakers that are playing music and avoid sitting under them. A booth or table near a wall can provide quieter conditions.

In chapter seven: People and Places, you will learn in-depth how to analyze frequent locations to optimize your access.

Video Calling Apps

For some people, it may be easier to use video calling apps like FaceTime, Zoom, Google Meet, etc. This can give you the benefit of seeing the other person's facial expressions, lips, and gestures as opposed to just using a voice call. People who rely on sign language to communicate on the phone use video calling apps to converse with other signers.

Video Relay

Videophones are used to make phone calls in American Sign Language (ASL). Video Relay Services (VRS) provide ASL interpreters to interpret the call between ASL and English (or other spoken languages depending on the vendor.)

Notetakers

If you are attending a class or important work training session, and you need to take notes, using a notetaker will allow you to maintain your visual attention to the speaker so you can lip read and take advantage of other visual cues such as gestures and facial expressions. If you set this up yourself, ask someone that you trust to take thorough notes. If you are taking a university course, the office for students with disabilities can usually arrange this for you. Please note, if you are using a captioning service as an accommodation, you can also ask if you are allowed to keep the transcript for future reference.

Alert Signal Devices

There are a variety of devices on the market that can alert you to important sounds in your home or in your environment. These can use visual signals (flashing lights) and tactile signals (vibration). Alarm clocks come equipped with a bed shaker you can place under your pillow or mattress to wake you. Other devices alert you to a baby cry, carbon monoxide alarm, smoke alarm, doorbell, telephone ring, and severe weather. You can find vendors by asking your local disability resource office or searching on the internet. Smartphones and smartwatches can provide visual and tactile (vibration) alerts you can set for certain sounds and use the timer function in place of common appliance timers (oven, microwave, dryer.)

Check out hearingoutloud.net for links to many alert device vendors.

Hearing Dogs

Hearing service dogs are another option for alerting you to sounds by making physical contact (pawing, jumping on, or nosing you) then leading you to the sound. Sometimes, our pets already have a keen sense of alerting us to sounds we can't hear; however, a service dog for the deaf/hard of hearing requires very specialized training not only to alert you to important sounds, but they also must have excellent behavioral skills in a variety of public situations.

Check out hearingoutloud.net for a list of reputable facilities for hearing service dogs.

ACCOMMODATIONS & ASSISTIVE TECHNOLOGY
JOURNAL ACTIVITY

What accommodations or assistive technology could help you that you haven't tried yet? Why not? If assertiveness is holding you back, you will learn new strategies in chapter seven: People and Places. Create an action plan for any new accommodations you would like to try. Who do you need to talk to? If you want to try a new piece of assistive technology, where will you find it? Do you need financial assistance to obtain it?

_____

_____

_____

_____

_____

_____

_____

_____

_____

_____

_____

_____

_____

_____

_____

_____

_____

_____

7 | people and places

Section One

Welcome to chapter seven: People and Places. In this section, we'll go over the goals for this chapter. We will begin with a journal activity, then discuss the foundational concepts of this chapter including the that idea hearing loss is really a communication loss, and an important reminder: there is no need to apologize.

Chapter 7 Goals:

- I understand hearing loss is actually a communication loss occurring between two or more people. I am not the only person responsible for my understanding.
- I have multiple ways to self-disclose my hearing loss based on the person and situation.
- I can ask for the accommodations I need.
- I can educate my conversation partner about effective communication strategies to support my understanding.
- I can initiate communication repair strategies in a direct and clear manner.

- I can effectively and respectfully refute accusations of "selective hearing" and only hearing when I "want" to.
- I can analyze listening environments to determine what factors make the space challenging to hear, understand, and feel included.
- I can create an action plan to effectively address a challenging listening environment so I can actively participate.
- I can confidently and gracefully turn down participation in certain environments if they are unpleasant or too much of a struggle.
- I know there are laws written to protect my rights for accessibility and inclusion, and I know who to contact if I need help.

PEOPLE-Introduction

In the work you completed in chapter five: Identity and Self-Love, you spent a significant amount of time and energy contemplating how your hearing loss is part of your identity and how to practice self-acceptance. We also talked about the importance of self-disclosure and the language you use to tell people about your hearing loss. As we begin chapter 7: People & Places, please keep in mind the power of self-acceptance: you are more than your hearing loss, and your hearing loss is a part of who you are. When you interact with the people in your life, owning your hearing loss, developing assertiveness skills, and standing up for what you need will only improve your self-esteem and confidence.

Hearing Loss is Communication Loss

Hearing loss is unique among the different types of disabilities because it directly affects both your and the other person's ability to easily communicate. Your hearing loss is not just "your problem"--in order to have successful communication, it impacts the people with whom you interact. Hearing loss actually is a communication loss. Difficulty hearing creates difficulty communicating. Communication is a two-way street, with both communication partners responding to each other. You can either pretend you understand when you really don't, or tell the other person about your hearing loss. Telling the other person about it is powerful because it creates the opportunity for them to pull their own weight.

No Need to Apologize

Having a hearing loss is simply a fact of your life. You didn't ask for it, you didn't do anything to deserve it, and you didn't fall out of bed one day looking for it. It is what it is. However, it is incredibly common for people with hearing loss to say, "I'm sorry," "pardon me," and "excuse me" because we feel it's the polite thing to say. The people you run into day in and day out, who may not know anyone with a hearing loss, carry countless misconceptions about it. If people can see them, they may wrongly assume your hearing aids or cochlear implant processors have "corrected" your hearing, especially if you have relatively clear speech. When you've missed something and you apologize, you inadvertently reinforce the misconception that you alone carry the burden of understanding them, as if you dropped the ball and are now apologizing because you didn't pay enough attention or you didn't focus enough on their words or you didn't turn up the volume enough. You can confidently address communication breakdowns in a variety of ways, which we will cover in this chapter, but it's an imperfect situation which is clearly not your fault, so there's no need to apologize.

WHO ARE MY PEOPLE?
JOURNAL ACTIVITY

You are going to create a picture of the people in your life. Use the instructions below to complete the diagram.

Step One: In the inner circle, write the names of your closest family members and friends. These are the people with whom you spend most of your time socially. You probably celebrate their birthdays, spend holidays together, and they know you better than most people.

Step Two: In the next circle, write the names of people you see frequently but not intimately. They might be your coworkers, neighbors, or are friends of your closest family and friends. You probably see them in a few social situations and you comfortably chat about a variety of topics with them.

Step Three: In the next circle, write the names of people in your life who function primarily in a professional way. They may be your doctor, your pharmacist, your child's teacher, your boss, your mail carrier. You interact with them primarily in the professional capacity of their occupation, but you see them on a somewhat regular basis.

Step Four: In the outermost circle, write the titles or short descriptions of typical strangers with whom you interact on a limited basis. These might be a bus driver, a grocery clerk, bank teller, furnace repair technician, or a person you meet at the dog park. Your interactions with these people are usually brief but occasionally involve important information exchanges.

We will use this diagram as we move through this chapter.

Who Are My People?

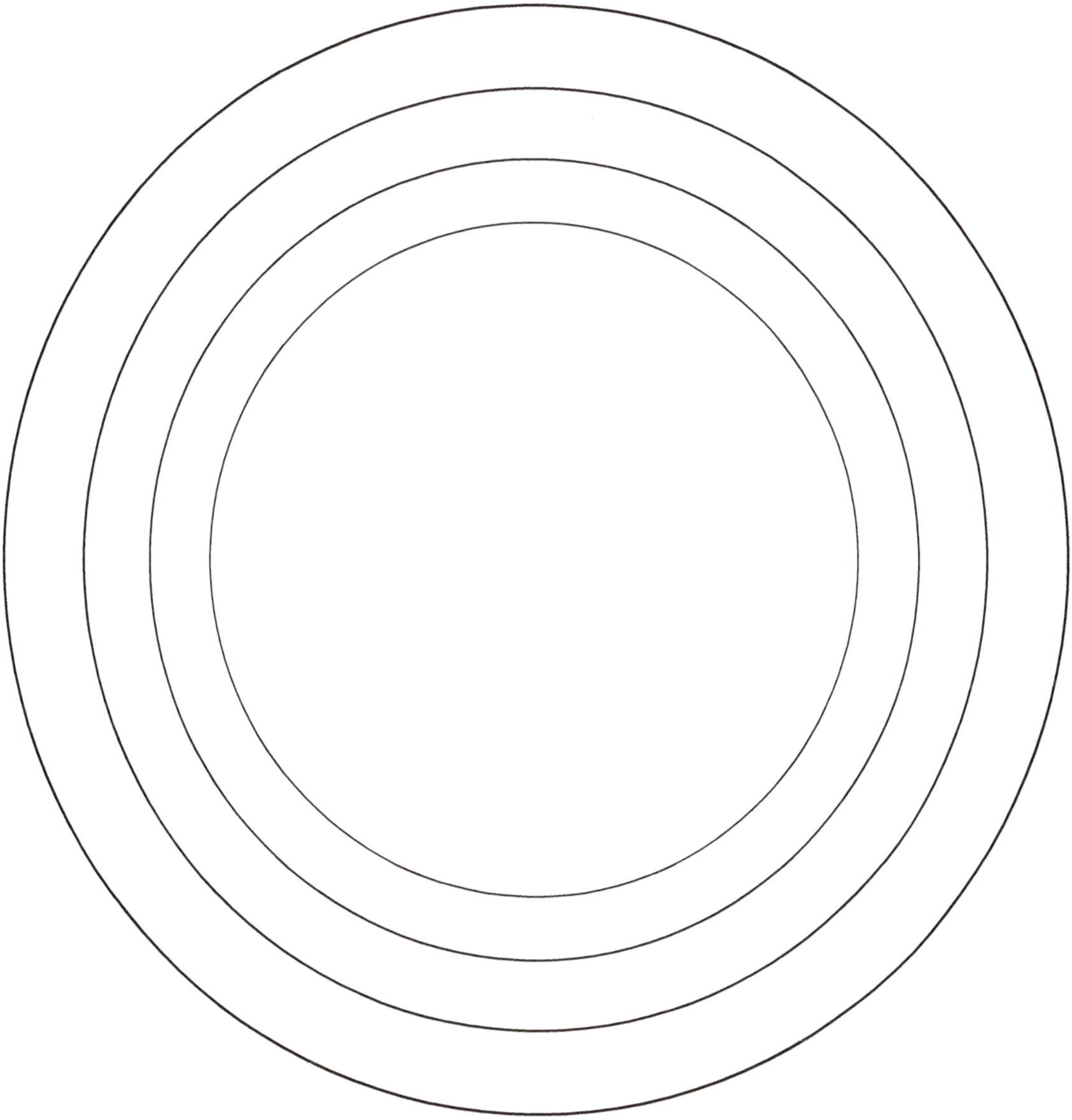

Section Two

In this section, we will deep dive into self-disclosure and the many different ways you may choose to do this.

Self-Disclosure

If you don't wear hearing technology, or yours isn't immediately noticeable, hearing loss is an invisible disability. Invisible disabilities make getting the accommodations you need even more difficult because it involves a constant revolving door of self-disclosure. Self-disclosure is vitally important for you to get what you need in order to have equal access to information and to benefit from enriching conversations with others. There are a multitude of ways you can tell someone about your hearing loss, and the words you use may depend on the person with whom you are talking and the situation.

Nonverbal Self-Disclosure

Think of the disabilities requiring an aid making the disability instantly apparent, such as the use of a wheelchair or white cane. In these cases, self-disclosure isn't immediately necessary, and most people instinctively know how to provide basic accommodations, such as stepping out of the way or offering assistance.

Your personal hearing technology (hearing aids or cochlear implant processors) might be easily visible and a simple finger point to them can clue them in. Unfortunately, people don't always recognize what you're pointing to. There is a wide variety of electronics people wear on their ears, and so a hearing aid or cochlear implant may not indicate clearly you have a hearing loss.

Tattoos, another form of nonverbal self-disclosure, can also reinforce your pride in your identity. A popular one is the "mute" symbol placed behind an ear.

Many people, especially during the pandemic, choose to wear a button or article of clothing stating "I have hearing loss" and require accommodations. This kind of nonverbal self-disclosure may be effective in an occupational setting where you encounter many strangers, such as a store clerk or restaurant server. When you are directly communicating with so many people, a quick reference to a button or t-shirt indicating "hard of hearing" or "deaf" or "I read lips" or "I use sign language" can make the interaction a little smoother. A quick search on Etsy.com will turn up a variety of products including this kind of personalization. A word of caution here, in certain locations or situations (on a walking path, bus station, etc) wearing something identifying you as unable to hear may put you in a vulnerable position.

Brief Self-Disclosure

A brief disclosure is a short couple of words meant to get the most essential information across easily and quickly and are usually for the people in your outermost circle—strangers. Look back in your journal to My Words (page 118). Here you decided on words to easily describe your hearing loss in a way sensible to you. These may be the words you use in your brief disclosure.

Technical Self-Disclosure

A technical disclosure will include more detailed information about the specific kind of hearing loss you have. Recall learning about ear anatomy and how to read your audiogram in chapter three. Using this information, your technical disclosure will include the stability, laterality, degree, and configuration of your hearing loss. You may also include the technical details of your hearing history, such as surgeries and types of hearing technology you've used. This type of disclosure is likely what you'll use when speaking with an audiologist, others with hearing loss, a speech pathologist, or other professionals with background knowledge in hearing loss.

Expanded Self-Disclosure

More than a brief disclosure, the expanded disclosure provides more information such as how you functionally hear, how your hearing technology works, what sounds are most difficult, or how background noise interferes with speech understanding. You might use this type of disclosure with people in the second circle: those you see frequently, such as coworkers, neighbors and friends. They know about your hearing loss, but will benefit from a better understanding of your hearing loss. Looking back to My Hearing Loss (pages 64-67) may be helpful in thinking about what to include in your expanded disclosure.

Emotional Self-Disclosure

The emotional disclosure provides the details of your hearing loss, the same as the expanded disclosure, and also includes your thoughts, feelings, preferences, ambitions, hopes, and fears about how it impacts your life emotionally. This is a longer conversation where you share more intimately the struggles you've experienced (refer to Processing Negative Experiences on pages 71-73), your feelings about stigma, and your path from impairment to empowerment.

The emotional self-disclosure is important to share with the closest people in your life. Maybe you haven't taken the time to really think about how you share your experience with the people most important to you. Do they truly understand how your hearing loss has impacted your emotional well-being? Do they know hearing loss isn't just difficulty hearing but it is difficulty communicating, and the effort required takes its toll?

It's important to put thought into the ways in which you self-disclose your hearing loss. It will vary depending on who you speak to, and you may already have situations or people in mind matching a particular type of self-disclosure.

SELF-DISCLOSURE KIT
JOURNAL ACTIVITY

Jot down your thoughts, ideas, and drafts for each type of self-disclosure we have gone over in this chapter. If you have particular settings or people matching the type of disclosure you've drafted, add their names or descriptions. Once you've completed each type of self-disclosure, take some time to refine and rehearse them.

Write out the actual words you will say when you need to self-disclose and then rehearse them. Visualize yourself standing or sitting confidently and imagine yourself saying the words directly and without apology.

Nonverbal Self-Disclosure

_____

_____

_____

_____

_____

_____

_____

Brief Self-Disclosure

_____

_____

_____

_____

_____

_____

Self-Disclosure Kit

Technical Self-Disclosure

_____
_____
_____
_____
_____
_____
_____
_____
_____
_____
_____
_____
_____
_____
_____
_____
_____
_____
_____
_____
_____
_____
_____
_____

Self-Disclosure Kit

Expanded Self-Disclosure

_____
_____
_____
_____
_____
_____
_____
_____
_____
_____
_____
_____
_____
_____
_____
_____
_____
_____
_____
_____
_____
_____
_____
_____
_____

Self-Disclosure Kit

Emotional Self-Disclosure

_____
_____
_____
_____
_____
_____
_____
_____
_____
_____
_____
_____
_____
_____
_____
_____
_____
_____
_____
_____
_____
_____
_____
_____
_____

Self-Disclosure Kit

_____
_____
_____
_____
_____
_____
_____
_____
_____
_____
_____
_____
_____
_____
_____
_____
_____
_____
_____
_____
_____
_____
_____
_____
_____
_____

Section Three

In this section you will be immersed in empowering self-advocacy strategies!

Teaching People How to Treat You

Every interaction you have with someone is an opportunity to provide a lesson on how to treat you. If you have known a person for a long time, think about how this person has learned to communicate with you. Are they aware of conditions which make hearing more difficult for you? Have you apologized frequently for misunderstanding something they've said and might they have learned to be annoyed with you (i.e. blame you) for not hearing? When they fail to communicate clearly, has your frustration taught them what to do, or what not to do? Regardless of the patterns already established in your relationships, you have new opportunities every interaction to teach them how to treat you moving forward.

For a hearing person, communicating with a person who has a hearing loss is not always intuitive, and the strategies that work are significantly different than how they interact in the larger hearing world. The skills needed for communication with someone who has a hearing loss are not universal and people may assume because you have a hearing loss and so does their grandmother, the way they adapt their communication should be the same even though this is not necessarily the case. Remember, the expectations in hearing society are communication is to be quick, invisible, and effective, and the assumptions about hearing aids and cochlear implants are they can essentially fix a hearing loss. When breakdowns occur, people are better able to provide what you need when you actually tell them what you need.

Communication with a hard of hearing or deaf person requires intentionality and awareness. I encourage you to see the blessing in this. In a world where our attentions are infinitely divided and distracted as we multitask, slowing down in mindful communication with another person creates a more effective and meaningful connection.

Communication Strategies and Communication Repair

In addition to hearing aids, cochlear implants, assistive listening devices, accommodations or other technology, there are simple but impactful communication strategies that make conversation easier. You are probably aware of many and know they can significantly help you hear and understand. The challenge is asking for what you need. This is called self-advocacy, which is defined by the National Deaf Center as "the ability to articulate one's needs and make informed decisions about the support necessary to meet those needs."

It is far more effective to tell people what you need (i.e. "speak clearly," and "I need to see your face,") than to tell them what's wrong (such as "I can't hear you," "you are mumbling,") or what not to do (including "don't whisper," "don't shout.") The more specific and efficient your suggestions, the easier it will be for them to do what you ask. Consider replacing "what?" and "huh?" with "say that again?" and "what did you say about the (insert topic)?"

The goal is to have quick, clear, easy and concise phrases for you to say. It's up to you if you want to include polite words in your requests. You can easily drop in a "please" and a "thank you" to any of your phrases. Here are a few highly effective suggestions.

Common Effective Communication Requests

"Speak clearly."

"You need to have my full attention before speaking to me."

"I need to see your face."

"Speak to me only when we're in the same room."

"Speak up," or "speak louder."

"Speak without gum or food in your mouth."

"Trim your mustache and/or beard so I can see your lips."

"Turn down the TV/radio/music and say that again?"

Common Communication Repair Requests

"Repeat what you said," or "Say that again?"

"Rephrase what you said."

"Simplify what you said."

Specific word request: "I heard x, y and z, but I missed ___."

TEACHING PEOPLE
HOW TO TREAT ME
JOURNAL ACTIVITY

ASKING FOR ACCOMMODATIONS

Thinking about the technology and accommodations you learned about in chapter six: Technology and Accommodations, are there devices or accommodations you would like to request? How will you ask for it? Plan the specific words you will use to ask for what you need. Rehearse them until you feel comfortable and confident with the words.

_____

_____

_____

_____

_____

_____

_____

_____

_____

_____

_____

_____

_____

_____

_____

_____

_____

TEACHING COMMUNICATION STRATEGIES

What communication strategies are essential to your understanding? How will you inform and teach your communication partner what you need? Clear and concise works best. Rehearse them until you feel comfortable and confident with the words.

_____

_____

_____

_____

_____

_____

_____

_____

_____

_____

_____

_____

_____

_____

_____

_____

_____

_____

_____

_____

Teaching People How to Treat Me

COMMUNICATION REPAIR

Consider the different ways to repair a communication breakdown. How are they different from, "huh?" and "what?" Are there more concise phrases to communicate the specific information you are missing? Rehearse them until you feel comfortable and confident with the words.

_____

_____

_____

_____

_____

_____

_____

_____

_____

_____

_____

_____

_____

_____

_____

_____

_____

_____

_____

Practicing and visualizing the words and phrases you will use in these situations will build your self-confidence. Drop the apologies and vague statements of annoyance. Confidently self-disclosing your hearing loss, directly requesting accommodations, clearly stating communication strategies specific to your needs, and overtly implementing communication repair requests is what creates an empowered self-advocate.

Section Four

In this section we dismantle the term "selective hearing" and arm you with powerful information to refute this kind of accusation in the future.

A Word About "Selective Hearing"

People with hearing loss often get accused of having "selective hearing" or only hearing when they "want to." Someone saying this about you can be painful because it characterizes your hearing loss as a condition that worsens or improves based on your motivation regarding the statement said. This implies you may be pretending not to hear requests or comments you feel are undesirable. For example, when a parent asked you to clean your room and you didn't hear it, but they also said it was time for dinner and you understood the message easily, there are a lot of factors in play.

Because our brain relies on many external cues to fill in missed auditory information, context and timing play a big role in understanding. For most messages, the cognitive energy exerted to understand spoken language is significantly higher than a typical hearing person.

If you were in your office around 5:30 pm and you could smell something cooking in the kitchen and you heard, "Ime –er" the logical conclusion after filling in the blanks is, "Time for dinner!"

If it's 9:30 am on a Saturday morning and you hear, "--oom!" without additional context, the message could be, "I'm on a Zoom call," "where's the broom?" or, "clean the bathroom."

Additionally, it is likely if you are not focusing your attention on what is said, the words don't have meaning and can sound almost like gibberish.

Focusing your attention on spoken language is called auditory attention and it requires active mental engagement in a way many hearing people don't understand. You probably have naturally learned how to do this, and might not even realize it, but after engaging your auditory attention in a challenging listening environment, you are exhausted.

This is called listening fatigue and it is a very real experience. We will discuss this further in chapter eight: Self-Care, but for now, it is important for you to understand what this is, and be able to explain it to the important people in your life.

"Selective hearing" is actually better explained as "selective auditory attention." The times you may have been accused of having selective hearing were probably times when the person talking to you failed to secure your full attention before speaking. Clearly and confidently insisting on this common communication strategy teaches the person how to effectively communicate with you with respect and appreciation for your hearing loss and the extra effort you must exert to understand them.

"SELECTIVE HEARING" REFLECTION
JOURNAL ACTIVITY

How did it feel to learn about "selective" hearing, listening fatigue, and auditory attention? Are there people in your life needing to hear this message? How will you effectively and respectfully communicate it to them?

_____

_____

_____

_____

_____

_____

_____

_____

_____

_____

_____

_____

_____

_____

_____

_____

_____

_____

Section Five

In this final section of chapter seven, you will learn how to deeply analyze frequent places and experiences and determine new strategies to improve your accessibility.

PLACES - Introduction

Every new location you enter is its own unique listening environment. There are many factors impacting how well or how little you can hear and understand while in them. Considering these factors and analyzing the physical environment ahead of time allows you to make a plan to ensure you have the best access possible. Sometimes, a very frustrating setting can be improved if you take a few minutes to think about the sources of frustration and any changes you could make in the future. For particularly difficult environments, bringing this information to your audiologist may prompt programming changes to your devices, or a suggestion for an accessory. Perhaps in a few instances, by considering all the options, you may determine a certain location is just not enjoyable and therefore no longer a place you would like to visit.

In the following pages, an entire section titled, "My Places" includes multiple copies of a form guiding you as you determine your listening needs in various places. To easily reference them again, a table of contents is available on the first page to jot down the name of the places you analyze in the forms. A list of suggested locations is also available. For now, choose one to complete, then continue the section on the page immediately following the *My Places* section of the book.

If you need to see an example of a completed journal entry for this activity, see page 226.

MY PLACES
JOURNAL ACTIVITY

MY PLACES - TABLE OF CONTENTS

	Description of Place
1	
2	
3	
4	
5	
6	
7	
8	
9	
10	

MY PLACES - PLACE SUGGESTIONS

- in a therapist's office
- a bar
- in the car
- in the kitchen
- in the bedroom
- when watching TV
- outside
- at work
- online
- in a small store
- in the grocery store
- in a large box store
- at the shopping mall
- in a restaurant
- on a walk
- walking with more than one person
- at the gym
- in the classroom (as a student)
- in a doctor's office
- as a presenter/speaker/teacher
- at the beach
- at the pool
- when camping
- around the fire pit
- on the bus
- at the airport
- on a boat
- on a train
- when gardening
- attending a sports event
- at the movie theater
- on a run
- on a bike ride
- at a hotel

Place: _____

```
┌─────────────────────────────────────────────────────────────────────┐
│                                                                     │
│                                                                     │
│                                                                     │
│                                                                     │
│                                                                     │
│                                                                     │
│                                                                     │
│                                                                     │
│                                                                     │
│                                                                     │
│                                                                     │
│                                                                     │
└─────────────────────────────────────────────────────────────────────┘
```

Map out main features of the location. Mark sources of interfering noise with an "X" or star.

Lighting: bright, normal, dim, dark, flashing, backlighting, _____

Acoustics: clear, echo-y, windy, sudden bursts, _____

Number of People: me, 2, small group 3-5, medium group 6-10, large group 11-20, crowd 20+ _____

Background Noise: silent, murmur, chatter, commotion, ruckus, roar, _____

Main Players:

_____ Speech: high, low, quiet, loud, mumbles, fast, facial hair, _____

_____ Speech: high, low, quiet, loud, mumbles, fast, facial hair, _____

_____ Speech: high, low, quiet, loud, mumbles, fast, facial hair, _____

_____ Speech: high, low, quiet, loud, mumbles, fast, facial hair, _____

_____ Speech: high, low, quiet, loud, mumbles, fast, facial hair, _____

Communication Mode: entertainment, instructional, informational, intimate, conversational, practical, other:

_____

What main factors make this space challenging for you to hear, understand, and feel included?

Use a highlighter or pen to circle them.

What changes could be made that would help you enjoy the activity and space?

_____

_____

Is there assistive listening technology or accommodations that could be helpful?
Remote mic, new program on hearing aid/cochlear implant processor, auto-caption app on my phone, real time
captioning service, change seating, other:

_____

_____

What could my main player(s) do to help me hear, understand and feel included?

_____

_____

Are there safety concerns? hearing protection, visual alerts for emergency situations, medic alert to inform
emergency workers of your needs, other:

_____

_____

Action plan:

_____

_____

_____

Let it go?

_____

_____

Place: _____

```
┌─────────────────────────────────────────────────────────────────────┐
│                                                                     │
│                                                                     │
│                                                                     │
│                                                                     │
│                                                                     │
│                                                                     │
│                                                                     │
│                                                                     │
│                                                                     │
│                                                                     │
└─────────────────────────────────────────────────────────────────────┘
```

Map out main features of the location. Mark sources of interfering noise with an "X" or star.

Lighting: bright, normal, dim, dark, flashing, backlighting, _____

Acoustics: clear, echo-y, windy, sudden bursts, _____

Number of People: me, 2, small group 3-5, medium group 6-10, large group 11-20, crowd 20+ _____

Background Noise: silent, murmur, chatter, commotion, ruckus, roar, _____

Main Players:

_____ Speech: high, low, quiet, loud, mumbles, fast, facial hair, _____

_____ Speech: high, low, quiet, loud, mumbles, fast, facial hair, _____

_____ Speech: high, low, quiet, loud, mumbles, fast, facial hair, _____

_____ Speech: high, low, quiet, loud, mumbles, fast, facial hair, _____

_____ Speech: high, low, quiet, loud, mumbles, fast, facial hair, _____

Communication Mode: entertainment, instructional, informational, intimate, conversational, practical, other:

_____

What main factors make this space challenging for you to hear, understand, and feel included?

Use a highlighter or pen to circle them.

What changes could be made that would help you enjoy the activity and space?

_____

_____

Is there assistive listening technology or accommodations that could be helpful?
Remote mic, new program on hearing aid/cochlear implant processor, auto-caption app on my phone, real time captioning service, change seating, other:

_____

_____

What could my main player(s) do to help me hear, understand and feel included?

_____

_____

Are there safety concerns? hearing protection, visual alerts for emergency situations, medic alert to inform emergency workers of your needs, other:

_____

_____

Action plan:

_____

_____

_____

Let it go?

_____

_____

Place: _____

```

```

Map out main features of the location. Mark sources of interfering noise with an "X" or star.

Lighting: bright, normal, dim, dark, flashing, backlighting, _____

Acoustics: clear, echo-y, windy, sudden bursts, _____

Number of People: me, 2, small group 3-5, medium group 6-10, large group 11-20, crowd 20+ _____

Background Noise: silent, murmur, chatter, commotion, ruckus, roar, _____

Main Players:

_____ Speech: high, low, quiet, loud, mumbles, fast, facial hair, _____

_____ Speech: high, low, quiet, loud, mumbles, fast, facial hair, _____

_____ Speech: high, low, quiet, loud, mumbles, fast, facial hair, _____

_____ Speech: high, low, quiet, loud, mumbles, fast, facial hair, _____

_____ Speech: high, low, quiet, loud, mumbles, fast, facial hair, _____

Communication Mode: entertainment, instructional, informational, intimate, conversational, practical, other:

_____

What main factors make this space challenging for you to hear, understand, and feel included?

Use a highlighter or pen to circle them.

What changes could be made that would help you enjoy the activity and space?

_____

_____

Is there assistive listening technology or accommodations that could be helpful?
Remote mic, new program on hearing aid/cochlear implant processor, auto-caption app on my phone, real time captioning service, change seating, other:

_____

_____

What could my main player(s) do to help me hear, understand and feel included?

_____

_____

Are there safety concerns? hearing protection, visual alerts for emergency situations, medic alert to inform emergency workers of your needs, other:

_____

_____

Action plan:

_____

_____

_____

Let it go?

_____

_____

Place: _____

```



```

Map out main features of the location. Mark sources of interfering noise with an "X" or star.

Lighting: bright, normal, dim, dark, flashing, backlighting, _____

Acoustics: clear, echo-y, windy, sudden bursts, _____

Number of People: me, 2, small group 3-5, medium group 6-10, large group 11-20, crowd 20+ _____

Background Noise: silent, murmur, chatter, commotion, ruckus, roar, _____

Main Players:

_____ Speech: high, low, quiet, loud, mumbles, fast, facial hair, _____

_____ Speech: high, low, quiet, loud, mumbles, fast, facial hair, _____

_____ Speech: high, low, quiet, loud, mumbles, fast, facial hair, _____

_____ Speech: high, low, quiet, loud, mumbles, fast, facial hair, _____

_____ Speech: high, low, quiet, loud, mumbles, fast, facial hair, _____

Communication Mode: entertainment, instructional, informational, intimate, conversational, practical, other:

_____

What main factors make this space challenging for you to hear, understand, and feel included?

Use a highlighter or pen to circle them.

What changes could be made that would help you enjoy the activity and space?

_____

_____

Is there assistive listening technology or accommodations that could be helpful?
Remote mic, new program on hearing aid/cochlear implant processor, auto-caption app on my phone, real time captioning service, change seating, other:

_____

_____

What could my main player(s) do to help me hear, understand and feel included?

_____

_____

Are there safety concerns? hearing protection, visual alerts for emergency situations, medic alert to inform emergency workers of your needs, other:

_____

_____

Action plan:

_____

_____

_____

Let it go?

_____

_____

Place: _____

[blank box]

Map out main features of the location. Mark sources of interfering noise with an "X" or star.

Lighting: bright, normal, dim, dark, flashing, backlighting, _____

Acoustics: clear, echo-y, windy, sudden bursts, _____

Number of People: me, 2, small group 3-5, medium group 6-10, large group 11-20, crowd 20+ _____

Background Noise: silent, murmur, chatter, commotion, ruckus, roar, _____

Main Players:

_____ Speech: high, low, quiet, loud, mumbles, fast, facial hair, _____

_____ Speech: high, low, quiet, loud, mumbles, fast, facial hair, _____

_____ Speech: high, low, quiet, loud, mumbles, fast, facial hair, _____

_____ Speech: high, low, quiet, loud, mumbles, fast, facial hair, _____

_____ Speech: high, low, quiet, loud, mumbles, fast, facial hair, _____

Communication Mode: entertainment, instructional, informational, intimate, conversational, practical, other:

_____

What main factors make this space challenging for you to hear, understand, and feel included?

Use a highlighter or pen to circle them.

What changes could be made that would help you enjoy the activity and space?

_____

_____

Is there assistive listening technology or accommodations that could be helpful?
Remote mic, new program on hearing aid/cochlear implant processor, auto-caption app on my phone, real time captioning service, change seating, other:

_____

_____

What could my main player(s) do to help me hear, understand and feel included?

_____

_____

Are there safety concerns? hearing protection, visual alerts for emergency situations, medic alert to inform emergency workers of your needs, other:

_____

_____

Action plan:

_____

_____

_____

Let it go?

_____

_____

Place: _____

```



```

Map out main features of the location. Mark sources of interfering noise with an "X" or star.

Lighting: bright, normal, dim, dark, flashing, backlighting, _____

Acoustics: clear, echo-y, windy, sudden bursts, _____

Number of People: me, 2, small group 3-5, medium group 6-10, large group 11-20, crowd 20+ _____

Background Noise: silent, murmur, chatter, commotion, ruckus, roar, _____

Main Players:

_____ Speech: high, low, quiet, loud, mumbles, fast, facial hair, _____

_____ Speech: high, low, quiet, loud, mumbles, fast, facial hair, _____

_____ Speech: high, low, quiet, loud, mumbles, fast, facial hair, _____

_____ Speech: high, low, quiet, loud, mumbles, fast, facial hair, _____

_____ Speech: high, low, quiet, loud, mumbles, fast, facial hair, _____

Communication Mode: entertainment, instructional, informational, intimate, conversational, practical, other:

_____

What main factors make this space challenging for you to hear, understand, and feel included?

Use a highlighter or pen to circle them.

What changes could be made that would help you enjoy the activity and space?

_____

_____

Is there assistive listening technology or accommodations that could be helpful?
Remote mic, new program on hearing aid/cochlear implant processor, auto-caption app on my phone, real time captioning service, change seating, other:

_____

_____

What could my main player(s) do to help me hear, understand and feel included?

_____

_____

Are there safety concerns? hearing protection, visual alerts for emergency situations, medic alert to inform emergency workers of your needs, other:

_____

_____

Action plan:

_____

_____

_____

Let it go?

_____

_____

Place: _____

```
┌─────────────────────────────────────────────────────────────────┐
│                                                                 │
│                                                                 │
│                                                                 │
│                                                                 │
│                                                                 │
│                                                                 │
│                                                                 │
│                                                                 │
│                                                                 │
│                                                                 │
│                                                                 │
└─────────────────────────────────────────────────────────────────┘
```

Map out main features of the location. Mark sources of interfering noise with an "X" or star.

Lighting: bright, normal, dim, dark, flashing, backlighting, _____

Acoustics: clear, echo-y, windy, sudden bursts, _____

Number of People: me, 2, small group 3-5, medium group 6-10, large group 11-20, crowd 20+ _____

Background Noise: silent, murmur, chatter, commotion, ruckus, roar, _____

Main Players:

_____ Speech: high, low, quiet, loud, mumbles, fast, facial hair, _____

_____ Speech: high, low, quiet, loud, mumbles, fast, facial hair, _____

_____ Speech: high, low, quiet, loud, mumbles, fast, facial hair, _____

_____ Speech: high, low, quiet, loud, mumbles, fast, facial hair, _____

_____ Speech: high, low, quiet, loud, mumbles, fast, facial hair, _____

Communication Mode: entertainment, instructional, informational, intimate, conversational, practical, other:

_____

What main factors make this space challenging for you to hear, understand, and feel included?

Use a highlighter or pen to circle them.

What changes could be made that would help you enjoy the activity and space?

_____

_____

Is there assistive listening technology or accommodations that could be helpful?
Remote mic, new program on hearing aid/cochlear implant processor, auto-caption app on my phone, real time captioning service, change seating, other:

_____

_____

What could my main player(s) do to help me hear, understand and feel included?

_____

_____

Are there safety concerns? hearing protection, visual alerts for emergency situations, medic alert to inform emergency workers of your needs, other:

_____

_____

Action plan:

_____

_____

_____

Let it go?

_____

_____

Place: _____

_____

Map out main features of the location. Mark sources of interfering noise with an "X" or star.

Lighting: bright, normal, dim, dark, flashing, backlighting, _____

Acoustics: clear, echo-y, windy, sudden bursts, _____

Number of People: me, 2, small group 3-5, medium group 6-10, large group 11-20, crowd 20+ _____

Background Noise: silent, murmur, chatter, commotion, ruckus, roar, _____

Main Players:

_____ Speech: high, low, quiet, loud, mumbles, fast, facial hair, _____

_____ Speech: high, low, quiet, loud, mumbles, fast, facial hair, _____

_____ Speech: high, low, quiet, loud, mumbles, fast, facial hair, _____

_____ Speech: high, low, quiet, loud, mumbles, fast, facial hair, _____

_____ Speech: high, low, quiet, loud, mumbles, fast, facial hair, _____

Communication Mode: entertainment, instructional, informational, intimate, conversational, practical, other:

_____

What main factors make this space challenging for you to hear, understand, and feel included?

Use a highlighter or pen to circle them.

What changes could be made that would help you enjoy the activity and space?

_____

_____

Is there assistive listening technology or accommodations that could be helpful?
Remote mic, new program on hearing aid/cochlear implant processor, auto-caption app on my phone, real time captioning service, change seating, other:

_____

_____

What could my main player(s) do to help me hear, understand and feel included?

_____

_____

Are there safety concerns? hearing protection, visual alerts for emergency situations, medic alert to inform emergency workers of your needs, other:

_____

_____

Action plan:

_____

_____

_____

Let it go?

_____

_____

Place: _____

Map out main features of the location. Mark sources of interfering noise with an "X" or star.

Lighting: bright, normal, dim, dark, flashing, backlighting, _____

Acoustics: clear, echo-y, windy, sudden bursts, _____

Number of People: me, 2, small group 3-5, medium group 6-10, large group 11-20, crowd 20+ _____

Background Noise: silent, murmur, chatter, commotion, ruckus, roar, _____

Main Players:

_____ Speech: high, low, quiet, loud, mumbles, fast, facial hair, _____

_____ Speech: high, low, quiet, loud, mumbles, fast, facial hair, _____

_____ Speech: high, low, quiet, loud, mumbles, fast, facial hair, _____

_____ Speech: high, low, quiet, loud, mumbles, fast, facial hair, _____

_____ Speech: high, low, quiet, loud, mumbles, fast, facial hair, _____

Communication Mode: entertainment, instructional, informational, intimate, conversational, practical, other:

_____

What main factors make this space challenging for you to hear, understand, and feel included?

Use a highlighter or pen to circle them.

What changes could be made that would help you enjoy the activity and space?

_____

_____

Is there assistive listening technology or accommodations that could be helpful?
Remote mic, new program on hearing aid/cochlear implant processor, auto-caption app on my phone, real time captioning service, change seating, other:

_____

_____

What could my main player(s) do to help me hear, understand and feel included?

_____

_____

Are there safety concerns? hearing protection, visual alerts for emergency situations, medic alert to inform emergency workers of your needs, other:

_____

_____

Action plan:

_____

_____

_____

Let it go?

_____

_____

Place: _____

```



```

Map out main features of the location. Mark sources of interfering noise with an "X" or star.

Lighting: bright, normal, dim, dark, flashing, backlighting, _____

Acoustics: clear, echo-y, windy, sudden bursts, _____

Number of People: me, 2, small group 3-5, medium group 6-10, large group 11-20, crowd 20+ _____

Background Noise: silent, murmur, chatter, commotion, ruckus, roar, _____

Main Players:

_____ Speech: high, low, quiet, loud, mumbles, fast, facial hair, _____

_____ Speech: high, low, quiet, loud, mumbles, fast, facial hair, _____

_____ Speech: high, low, quiet, loud, mumbles, fast, facial hair, _____

_____ Speech: high, low, quiet, loud, mumbles, fast, facial hair, _____

_____ Speech: high, low, quiet, loud, mumbles, fast, facial hair, _____

Communication Mode: entertainment, instructional, informational, intimate, conversational, practical, other:

_____

What main factors make this space challenging for you to hear, understand, and feel included?

   Use a highlighter or pen to circle them.

What changes could be made that would help you enjoy the activity and space?

_____

_____

Is there assistive listening technology or accommodations that could be helpful?
Remote mic, new program on hearing aid/cochlear implant processor, auto-caption app on my phone, real time captioning service, change seating, other:

_____

_____

What could my main player(s) do to help me hear, understand and feel included?

_____

_____

Are there safety concerns? hearing protection, visual alerts for emergency situations, medic alert to inform emergency workers of your needs, other:

_____

_____

Action plan:

_____

_____

_____

Let it go?

_____

_____

Place: **Community Room at daughter's apt bldg**

Map out main features of the location. Mark sources of interfering noise with an "X" or star.

Lighting: bright, (normal) (dim,) dark, flashing, backlighting, **not very bright, few windows**

Acoustics: clean, (echo-y,) windy, sudden bursts, **large room, tall ceilings**

Number of People: me, 2, small group 3-5, (medium group 6-10,) large group 11-20, crowd 20+ _____

Background Noise: silent, murmur, (chatter,) commotion, ruckus, roar, **HVAC is loud**

Main Players:

Carol _____ Speech: high, low, (quiet,) loud, (mumbles,) fast, facial hair, _____

Christine, _____ Speech: high, low, quiet, loud, (mumbles) fast, facial hair, _____

Kids (4) _____ Speech: high, low, quiet, loud, mumbles, fast, facial hair **sometimes mumble**

Babies (2) _____ Speech: (high,) low, quiet, (loud,) mumbles, fast, facial hair, **Noisy!** (or look away)

_____ Speech: high, low, quiet, loud, mumbles, fast, facial hair, _____

Communication Mode: entertainment, instructional, informational, intimate, (conversational,) practical, other:
informal family gathering, games, food

What main factors make this space challenging for you to hear, understand, and feel included?
Use a highlighter or pen to circle them. **Seating is too spaced out**

What changes could be made that would help you enjoy the activity and space?

Use the seating around area rug, go outside, remind everyone, one speaker at a time!

Is there assistive listening technology or accommodations that could be helpful?
Remote mic, new program on hearing aid/cochlear implant processor, auto-caption app on my phone, real time captioning service, change seating, other:

remote mic might help, buts lots of commotion during games that were physically active

What could my main player(s) do to help me hear, understand and feel included?

One speaker at a time, make sure seated where I can see your face, repeat when I ask (without hesitation)

Are there safety concerns? hearing protection, visual alerts for emergency situations, medic alert to inform emergency workers of your needs, other:

No

Action plan:

Next time pre-discuss my needs, change hearing aid setting to see if it improves in echo-y space, adjust my location more.

Let it go?

No! I just needs a few tweaks!

A Word About Your Rights

It is important to know your rights as a person with a hearing disability. As an adult in the US, there are two main laws written to protect you in most public places, schools, and the workplace.

Section 504 of the Rehabilitation Act of 1973 is a federal civil rights law to stop discrimination against people with disabilities. If you are otherwise qualified, section 504 provides access to federally funded jobs, programs, and activities without discrimination based solely on disability. This includes virtually all universities, colleges, and career training programs since most of them receive federal assistance (i.e. money from taxpayers). This also includes employers, such as hospitals, nursing homes, and public schools, who receive federal assistance. Providing access means you can't be turned away because of your hearing loss if you otherwise meet the requirements for admission to a program or the job position. It also means you are entitled to accommodations, such as captioning, notetakers, sign language interpreters, and assistive listening devices, as needed to obtain equal access to the programs and services.

The Americans with Disabilities Act (ADA) passed in 1990 prohibits discrimination against people with disabilities in several areas, including employment, transportation, public accommodations, communications and access to state and local government' programs and services. It protects your rights to receive reasonable accommodations in most public places.

If you feel your rights to access are violated, there are a number of things you can do.

Check out hearingoutloud.net for helpful resource links.

Navigating the world with hearing loss can be tricky, but the strategies you've learned in this chapter will help you move about it with greater confidence. Self-disclosure and communication repair can be challenging and I hope the time you've invested thinking about how to approach them leaves you feeling empowered.

8 | self-care

Section One

Welcome to chapter eight: Self-Care. In this section, we will go over the goals for this chapter. Next we will discuss the foundational concepts for this chapter. Finally, you will learn about listening fatigue and strategies to combat it.

Chapter 8 Goals:

- I know what listening fatigue, self-disclosure fatigue, self-advocacy fatigue, and technology fatigue is and how to combat it in my life.
- I recognize bluffing comes at a cost.
- I can set healthy social and experiential boundaries that protect myself and my energy.
- I can recognize incidents of audism, ableism, and hearing privilege and how they have affected me.
- I have considered the value sign language can bring to my life.
- I know how to protect my residual hearing.
- I know the value of finding people who can relate to my experience as a person with hearing loss.

Introduction

Self-care is the thoughtful practice of protecting and improving your own well-being, physically and emotionally. Self-care includes intentional acts to nurture and replenish the body, mind, and soul. Generally speaking, eating well, exercising regularly, getting enough sleep, maintaining strong social connections, building financial security, and nurturing spiritual needs all fall under the self-care umbrella. While there are countless ways to approach self-care for all kinds of reasons, in this chapter we are going to focus on strategies specific to living with hearing loss.

As you have already learned, any degree of hearing loss can significantly impact social communication. The important relationships in your life can experience strain when communication breaks down.

It is important to have a toolbox of strategies you can use to replenish yourself when you experience fatigue due to hearing loss. In this chapter, you will learn about four types of fatigue unique to living with hearing loss, as well as some strategies to manage them.

Listening Fatigue

Hearing loss, of any degree, creates an excessive drain on your energy when you're conversing with people using spoken (vs. signed) language. You have probably noticed often after a social gathering or a day at work, your mind feels exhausted and you're craving quiet time, or an isolated activity such as listening to music or watching TV. This exhaustion is real, for a number of reasons, and knowing where it comes from can help you to choose mindful self-care strategies to replenish your mind and body.

Research has shown, when listening to a person speak, especially with background noise present, people with hearing loss experience an increased cognitive load causing the brain to work harder than people without hearing loss. Your brain must reallocate resources to compensate for a garbled auditory signal. Difficulty hearing reduces the activation of the primary auditory cortex, the area of the brain critical for sound processing. For people with hearing loss, there is an increased activation in the prefrontal cortex, the area of the brain responsible for language comprehension; this means your brain is expending extra energy filling in sounds and words you didn't hear. It does this by applying context clues, facial expressions, mouth shape, and other non-verbal cues. While your brain is preoccupied filling in the missing pieces of the puzzle, it has less energy available for comprehension and memory. All of this leads to reduced auditory memory (remembering what you heard,) reduced working memory (holding information short-term to perform a task, such as adding numbers,) and reduced ability to pay attention and understand what you hear. Listening fatigue is a very real experience, and it requires thoughtful self-care strategies to reenergize your brain with rest.

Combating Listening Fatigue

Finding activities you enjoy which do not require you to understand spoken language (and don't require you to respond) can give your brain a welcome reprieve from listening fatigue. A listening break can be anywhere from five minutes to an hour, depending on your schedule, amount of fatigue, and whether you are actively recovering from listening fatigue or proactively preparing for an especially noisy or demanding event.

There are a large number of activities to choose from. Choices deaf and hard of hearing people often make include taking a walk (with or without streaming or listening to music, podcasts, audiobooks), arts and craft projects (painting, drawing, sewing, knitting), watching television with captions, adult coloring books, scrolling social media, meditation, video games, and taking a nap.

There is a very important distinction between using these activities as a strategy to combat listening fatigue, and using these activities to avoid engaging in social or vocational activities. Be conscientious of your purpose and intentional of the time you engage in listening break activities. Your needs may vary from day to day.

COMBATING LISTENING FATIGUE
JOURNAL ACTIVITY

Consider times in the day you would benefit from a listening break. Brainstorm various ideas you'd like to try. Create an action plan to implement listening breaks into your daily life, and reflect on how it impacts your ability to attend and your mood.

_____
_____
_____
_____
_____
_____
_____
_____
_____
_____
_____
_____
_____
_____
_____
_____
_____
_____

Section Two

In this section, we will discuss self-disclosure fatigue and consider strategies to combat it.

Self-Disclosure Fatigue

Telling people you have a hearing loss is an important strategy to get the accommodations you need; however, it can also create stress, especially if it is something you have to do time and time again with many new people, or with people in your life who always seem to forget.

If you haven't had a lot of practice, self-disclosure can induce anxiety and self-doubt as you build the courage to do it. Your mind must process all the "what-ifs" you may be thinking: "What if they get annoyed? "What if they mock or tease me?" "What if it doesn't make any difference?" "What if they think I'm _____?" This can cause you to question the actual value of telling them and instead, find yourself putting it off, or simply bluffing.

Once you've told a person about your hearing loss, they may expect you to help them manage the feelings they have about your self-disclosure. They might respond with excessive sympathy: "Oh my! I don't know how you deal with that!" "Oh, it must be so sad not to hear music." "Oh no, I had no idea, I'm so sorry!" Or, they may express disbelief and suddenly insist on "testing" you by moving their mouth without speaking, or hiding their mouth behind their hand while saying something. You even might get questioned if you truly have a hearing loss because you don't wear hearing technology or because you can "speak well."

The purpose of self-disclosure is to inform people how they can improve your understanding of the conversation. Instead, after learning about your hearing loss, the person may derail the conversation by diverting into a side story about another person they know who has hearing loss, or the time they had such a bad head cold they couldn't hear for days, or take off on any number of other tangents. This is difficult to reign back in and the thought of interrupting them to make a request to speak up or talk a little slower increases the stress you may already feel.

You may find you need to frequently remind people in your life about your hearing loss and the accommodations you need. This repeated self-disclosure can be very frustrating and draining. You may feel, "If they truly cared, they wouldn't forget," or "If they truly cared, they would be actively thinking about how to make this situation easier for me right now." Often, the unfortunate reality is people are habitual creatures, and they tend to default to the behaviors most familiar to them. They may be very apologetic and vow to improve, but still fall short in the excitement of a party or heat of a conversation.

Combating Self-Disclosure Fatigue

As important as self-disclosure is, it can be a stressful experience for you. It's true what they say though about practice. It does make it easier. Planning ahead of time what you will do and say (as you did in chapter seven: People and Places) when faced with these situations is helpful. You may also want to consider non-verbal ways of informing people of your hearing loss (i.e. wearing a pin, visible and/or decorated hearing devices).

For people who repeatedly forget, and if this is a very important person in your life, having a conversation about this may be helpful. Entering the conversation, ensure you are approaching it with the desire to be understood and the other person is approaching it with the desire to be supportive and helpful. If either of you are feeling resentful, angry, or defensive, it is not the right time to have the conversation. Sharing how you feel in the situation is helpful. If you don't have the words for it, completing the Combating Self-Disclosure Fatigue journal activity may be useful if writing helps you communicate your emotions more clearly. During the conversation with this important person, you might agree on a prearranged, simple reminder cue you can use between you when the situation comes up again. Maybe this is a double tap on the shoulder or leg, or a gesture you make toward your ear. Whatever it is, it should quickly and easily trigger the other person's memory as to the strategies you agreed would be helpful in this situation.

COMBATING
SELF-DISCLOSURE FATIGUE
JOURNAL ACTIVITY

As you reflect on self-disclosure fatigue, write about your experiences and how they've impacted you. When you have a better understanding about how it has impacted your life, ask yourself: are there conversations you could have with people in your life who may have made self-disclosure difficult for you?

_____

_____

_____

_____

_____

_____

_____

_____

_____

_____

_____

_____

_____

_____

_____

_____

_____

_____

_____

Section Three

In this section, you will learn about self-advocacy fatigue and consider strategies to combat it.

Self-Advocacy Fatigue

As you learned in chapter seven: People & Places, self-advocacy usually immediately follows self-disclosure. Once you've shared your hearing loss status, teaching helpful strategies or requesting necessary accommodations comes next. Self-advocating can be difficult for any number of reasons. If you are lower in a social hierarchy than the person to whom you are talking, such as a boss or a professor, you may feel intimidated or worried you'll come across as pushy. If you have made requests for an accommodation and it isn't provided, you are forced to manage feelings of anger and annoyance while trying to problem solve how you will manage without the accommodation. If you are a naturally shy or introverted person, it feels against your very nature to speak up and ask for what you need.

The journey to becoming a good self-advocate isn't a simple process. It can be messy, filled with starts and stops, frustrations and triumphs. When you have a hearing loss it is almost always necessary to be a self-advocate, no matter where you are on your journey: prepared and confident, insecure and hesitant, or somewhere in between. Not self-advocating will leave you feeling isolated, ignored, and forgotten. There may be other people in your life who will try to advocate for you, and their support is definitely important; but in order to move through this world forming satisfying relationships and achieving purposeful goals that make you happy, you have to be able to say what you need. Just knowing this is true can feel overwhelming and exhausting. This is an extra expectation you wouldn't have if you didn't have this hearing loss. It is easy, and even justifiable, to feel resentful and angry about this. Those are valid feelings.

Once you've self-advocated and found it to be successful, you're not done. You will need to self-advocate again. And again. It will not be successful every time. Your request to be seated center toward the front at a comedy show so you can lip read worked last time, but this time, they gave the saved seat to another patron when you were running five minutes behind. Your request for captioned media in your class is taken care of every time, except the film being shown today–they forgot and they're so sorry. All eyes turn toward you as you fumble around saying, "Oh, um OK…," but honestly you're frustrated and embarrassed and just plain tired.

As is true with many other things in life, the old adage, "the squeaky wheel gets the grease," applies to self-advocacy. The more you do it, the more people will provide it. The more they provide it, the more it becomes part of their routine. Then, hopefully, the less of it you will have to do.

It is also true, even though you ask for it, and even though there are laws protecting and requiring your access to it, people, agencies and businesses will refuse to provide accommodations, and discrimination happens. When this happens, you are not in it alone. There are agencies and legal support available to back you up to provide full access where it is required by law. (Look back to chapter seven: People & Places for a review of the laws protecting your rights, as well as actions you can take to advocate for yourself in different scenarios. Unfortunately, this is not always a quick and easy process, but there are people who will fight on your behalf. Engaging in this level of self-advocacy, and advocacy for all people with hearing loss, can be exhausting but also rewarding. The law is on your side in most cases. If you have made accommodation requests which are refused, do not hesitate to reach out for support.

 Check out hearingoutloud.net for helpful resource links.

Combating Self-Advocacy Fatigue

Regardless of how often you have to do it, self-advocacy can be exhausting and it's important to recognize your feelings about it. Just as with self-disclosure, practice does make advocating for yourself easier and easier. Perhaps sending email requests versus talking directly to a person is the best way for you. Enlisting the help of a friend, an advisor, or a coworker, can make the job a little less daunting. You may need the help of a professional disability advocate or lawyer. Consider ways in which you can help others. Knowing you need to ask for help in the form of accommodations can feel less "needy" if you balance it with providing help and support for others. Remember, even though it can be uncomfortable, asking for and offering help is a pillar of self-care and a cornerstone to building community.

COMBATING
SELF-ADVOCACY FATIGUE
JOURNAL ACTIVITY

Write about your feelings about self-advocacy. It's ok if you feel resentful and angry about it–get it out. Consider ways self-advocacy can make you feel in control and confident.

_____

_____

_____

_____

_____

_____

_____

_____

_____

_____

_____

_____

_____

_____

_____

_____

_____

_____

_____

_____

Section Four

In this section, you will learn about technology fatigue and consider some strategies to combat it.

Technology Fatigue

In today's rapidly advancing technological world, devices meant to enhance our quality of life are constantly evolving. For hearing aid and cochlear implant users, these advancements bring huge improvements to sound quality, comfort, and connectivity. However, with these benefits comes an easily overlooked downside: technology fatigue. Technology fatigue is the physical and mental exhaustion that we experience when working with complex and constantly changing technology. For hearing aid and CI users, this fatigue can show up in several ways, impacting our overall well-being and the effectiveness of our devices.

Modern hearing aids and CIs are sophisticated pieces of technology. They now have features like Bluetooth connectivity, smartphone apps, noise-canceling algorithms, and even artificial intelligence to adapt to different sound environments automatically. While these features are designed to improve our listening experience, they also come with a level of complexity that can be overwhelming, especially for older users or those less familiar with modern technology.

For many of us, just learning to navigate the various settings, adjust volumes, and connect our hearing aids to other devices can be a daunting task. This learning curve is steep, and it requires a significant investment of time and mental energy. The frequent need for updates, troubleshooting connectivity issues, and keeping up with new software features can exacerbate the mental exhaustion.

We must often make quick decisions about when and how to use our devices, particularly in complex auditory environments. We may have pre programmed options installed on our devices, but we probably need to adjust or override these settings depending on our specific needs in different settings. This constant fiddling with tiny buttons or a slow-loading app can actually impose an added mental strain that comes from having to make adjustments when the speaker is already talking!

In addition to mental strain, there are physical aspects of technology fatigue that you likely experience. Modern hearing aids and CIs are generally designed to be comfortable, but they can still cause discomfort after prolonged use. Ear fatigue, headaches from continuous listening, and the discomfort of having a foreign object in the ear canal for extended periods can all contribute to a sense of physical fatigue.

Next, what about the maintenance of these devices? Regular cleaning, changing batteries or recharging, updating software, and troubleshooting any issues can become burdensome, especially if you also deal with limited dexterity or vision. When there is a problem we can't troubleshoot ourselves, we are faced with waiting days or weeks for an audiology appointment that may include an easy fix, or shipping your devices out for repair! You might not have a back up pair, so now what?

The psychological toll of technology fatigue can not be underestimated. You likely experience anxiety or frustration when faced with technical issues. This can even leave you feeling inadequate or dependent. Maybe it's the last straw, the deciding factor, that causes you to choose not to use your devices, completely undermining the benefits you deserve from them!

The rapid pace of technological advancement can stir up a sense of obsolescence. You might feel like your devices are outdated shortly after purchasing them, making you feel pressure to upgrade, which can be both financially and mentally taxing. This constant need to adapt to new technologies can cause you to feel as if you are never fully in control.

Combating Technology Fatigue

There is no doubt that technology fatigue can significantly impact you. Let's consider a few options that might help reduce this frustration.

Some manufacturers have improved their focus on user-friendly designs and intuitive interfaces that might help some of us. Clear, accessible instructions can help us feel more confident and in control of our devices. If you haven't made a purchase of devices yet, asking specifically for this may be something you want to discuss with your audiologist so they choose a manufacturer with excellent customer resources.

Personalized support and training should be made readily available. Reach out to your hearing care provider, make additional appointments, or send them messages, if you require assistance with your devices. Unfortunately, the problem is, audiologists and hearing aid specialists who could play a crucial role in helping us, often don't have the time, and so you could end up waiting weeks for an appointment. Another option may be to find a hearing loss support group, such as a local chapter of the Hearing Loss Association of America (HLAA), or a hearing loss buddy, that could give you better access to some peer education and support without feeling overwhelmed. You might ask a younger friend or family member who has more experience with advanced technology to help you troubleshoot or explain how something works. No shame here, it makes sense to seek out the "experts," and reaching out to them may spark a closer connection between the two of you. YouTube is another great resource. Search for how to videos using the specific brand and model of your devices and a brief description of the problem. Likely you'll find a video or two that provides some visuals and explanation for your problem. Leverage social media by joining groups which include others who use your same devices. Post your questions there and you'll probably find more than one person who has dealt with the problem before.

It is crucial to acknowledge the emotional and psychological aspects of technology fatigue. If you are feeling overwhelmed with technical issues, give yourself permission to walk away from it for a while. Allow yourself to create boundaries that might include a little more rest and self-care to address feeling anxious or frustration due to technology fatigue.

COMBATING TECHNOLOGY FATIGUE
JOURNAL ACTIVITY

What are your thoughts about technology fatigue? Is this something you've heard of before? Is it something that has been a source of stress? What ideas suggested in this section seem like they would be helpful? How can you alleviate some of that stress and get your technology needs taken care of?

Section Five

In this section we will consider the cost of bluffing, and also discuss the importance of setting boundaries.

The Cost of Bluffing

Bluffing is a strategy most of us with hearing loss have used. The word "bluff" is defined as "trying to deceive someone as to one's abilities or intentions." Nodding your head or laughing along with the crowd when you don't really know what was said is bluffing, and it can come at a cost to you and others.

When you bluff, it sends the message: "I heard and understood that." Bluffing too often can create the illusion your hearing is better than it actually is, and therefore, it will be more difficult to get people to modify their way of speaking or provide you with the accommodations you need. It can also backfire, making it obvious you didn't hear or understand because you can't answer a question about the topic you just bluffed you understood.

BLUFFING
JOURNAL ACTIVITY

Do you bluff often? When? And why? What are you missing because of it? When it's boiled down, bluffing is deception. How do you feel about deceiving others about your hearing loss? Thinking about what you've learned about self-disclosure and self-advocacy, can you use self-disclosure and self-advocacy statements to replace bluffing? How would this change your relationships and social interactions?

_____

_____

_____

_____

_____

_____

_____

_____

_____

_____

_____

_____

_____

_____

_____

_____

_____

_____

_____

_____

Creating Boundaries

Even though hearing loss creates barriers to communication and social interaction, your levels of fatigue due to a heavier cognitive load to understand speech, repeated self-disclosure and the constant need to self-advocate all contribute to the need for healthy boundaries.

A boundary is an imaginary line separating you and your energy from others and their demands on your energy. Without boundaries, people may take advantage of you and experiences may sap your energy because you haven't set limits about how you expect to be treated and how you will spend your energy. The purpose of setting boundaries is to protect your well-being. They can be rigid or loose—they are your boundaries, so you get to decide what they look like, and you can also change them as your needs change.

Social Boundaries

Social boundaries are the limits you establish in regard to with whom you choose to spend your time. You may set certain social boundaries for a few reasons. Completely out of your control, your particular hearing loss can dictate whose voices are easier to understand. There are likely people in your family or social circle who struggle to remember your hearing loss and rarely provide natural accommodations for you (facing you, not covering their mouth, etc). There may be people to whom you gravitate at certain gatherings and people you tend to avoid. You may have a friend or two who also have a hearing loss, and spending time with them allows you to feel validation and comfort in shared experiences.

Experiential Boundaries

Experiential boundaries are the limits you establish in regard to how you choose to spend your energy. When you think of all the different kinds of experiences you can have, all the different ways you can spend your time, consider what those experiences demand from you in terms of your auditory and visual attention, cognitive energy spent filling in blanks, and requirements for self-disclosure, self-advocacy and adaptation to the primary communication mode. Recall the work you did in chapter seven: People and Places where you analyzed locations for acoustics, lighting, sources of background noise, and so on. Experiential boundaries are similar, but are not restricted to a location. You may choose not to attend a music concert, regardless of location, because the noise level prevents you from enjoying the experience. You may choose not to attend a large party with more than 20 or 30 people, knowing it will be impossible to find a quiet area to talk with your friend. Or you may choose not to attend a dinner party because it's too difficult to lipread when everyone is eating. Instead, you may enjoy quietly listening to music with your partner or inviting a few friends over to lunch on your patio.

Keep in mind, there is an important distinction between using boundaries as a strategy to improve the quality of your life, and using boundaries to avoid engaging in valuable social or necessary vocational activities. Be conscientious of your purpose and intentional in the time you engage in both social and experiential boundaries.

BOUNDARIES
JOURNAL ACTIVITY

Consider any boundaries you may already have established, socially or experientially. Are they useful? Are there boundaries you haven't established but would like to consider? How would social or experiential boundaries improve your well-being?

_____
_____
_____
_____
_____
_____
_____
_____
_____
_____
_____
_____
_____
_____
_____
_____
_____
_____
_____
_____
_____

Section Six

In this final section of chapter eight, you will learn about audism, ableism and hearing privilege. After a journal activity, we'll touch on sign language, hearing protection, hearing technology jewelry, and finally finding your people. Then we will summarize your experiences in this book and wrap things up with a final journal entry reflecting on your thoughts and feelings having completed the journal.

Audism, Ableism, and Hearing Privilege

It is important for you to know about audism, ableism, and hearing privilege. As you move through life with a hearing loss, these topics will likely come up.

Audism is defined as discrimination or prejudice against individuals who are deaf or hard of hearing. Audism judges, labels, and limits individuals on the basis of whether a person hears and speaks.

Ableism is discrimination and social prejudice against people with disabilities based on the belief that typical abilities are superior. Both audism and ableism view a person with hearing loss or disability as less than those without hearing loss and without disability.

Hearing privilege is living life without facing common barriers that exist for d/Deaf and hard of hearing people. Examples are: being able to watch any movie regardless if it has closed captions, attending a doctor appointment without needing an interpreter, learning the nuances of spoken language easily, and easily going through a drive-thru without communication barriers.

AUDISM, ABLEISM, AND HEARING PRIVILEGE
JOURNAL ACTIVITY

Have you experienced audism or ableism because of your hearing loss? Describe those experiences and how they made you feel. Are there people in your life who don't understand the concept of hearing privilege, and if they did, would they better understand you? How can you counteract the impact these have had on your life? Are you inspired to become an activist?

_____
_____
_____
_____
_____
_____
_____
_____
_____
_____
_____
_____
_____
_____
_____
_____
_____
_____

Sign Language

There are many signed languages in the world. In the US, we use American Sign Language (ASL). ASL is a complete and robust language of its own, capable of communicating all the subtleties and nuances of the human experience. You may already know and use sign language. If not, you might consider learning it as a form of self-care. Using sign language is a powerful communication tool that does not rely on hearing or speaking. It is 100% visual, so it bypasses your hearing loss completely. Knowing sign language can open doors to the Deaf community, potentially offering you a new social network. Learning sign language with your partner and other loved ones will give you the opportunity to interact in a different way when hearing and spoken language fall short.

If you would like to learn sign language, it is highly recommended to learn from Deaf people. The value of learning from the Deaf community includes developing an appreciation for Deaf culture and its history, ensuring you receive accurate instruction in grammar, slang and local dialects, and financially supporting a person from the Deaf community. There are a few great resources on the internet to get you started.

Check out hearingoutloud.net for resource links.

Hearing Protection

If you have residual hearing, using hearing protection is an important form of self-care. Exposure to loud noise can cause irreversible damage to the stereocilia in the inner ear. (Look back at chapter three: Hearing Loss 101 to review hearing anatomy and noise induced hearing loss.) Invest in quality ear muffs, custom earplugs (ask your audiologist), or disposable foam earplugs. When you're in a noisy environment, try using an app on your phone to measure the decibel level. Increase your distance from a source of very loud noise. Keep the volume of your media at a reasonable level. Limit the amount of time you are exposed to loud noise. As a guideline, this table shows the amount of time exposed to a certain decibel level for hearing damage to occur.

85 dB: eight hours (hair dryer)

88 dB: four hours (food blender)

91 dB: two hours (motorcycle)

94 dB: one hour (rifle)

97 dB: 30 min (heavy traffic)

100 dB: 15 min (subway)

110 dB: two minutes (chainsaw)

130 dB: <one second (aircraft, explosives)

Hearing Technology Decoration

Acceptance of your hearing loss is important to your well-being. It allows you to learn the best ways to manage its effect on your life. There's another level beyond acceptance, and this is celebration. Not only do you accept you have a hearing loss, but you may have also decided to use hearing technology to improve your ability to communicate. To be clear, the use of hearing technology is a personal choice and whether you choose to use it or not is not inherently good or bad. But if you do choose to use it, why not celebrate it? Your hearing aids or cochlear implant processors are amazing pieces of technology you wear on your ears daily. As humans, we use color and print to actively express our individuality through our clothing, make up, hairstyle, eyewear, and footwear. Using color and print to decorate your hearing devices is another form of self-expression, reinforcing your feelings of acceptance, and offering a quick self-disclosure option. There are a variety of jewelry, stickers (often called "skins,"), fabrics with beading, and color options available. When purchasing new technology, ask your audiologist to show you the colors available for your devices, earmolds, tubing, and ear hooks.

Check out hearingoutloud.net for creative ways to dress up your hearing devices.

Find Your People

Finally, finding others who can relate to your experience is an important form of self-care. Imagine connecting and learning from another person living life with hearing loss. You may find you have a lot in common beyond hearing loss, and the value of knowing another person who "gets it" is priceless.

There are organizations you can join, such as the Hearing Loss Association of America, the National Association of the Deaf, the Association of Late-Deafened Adults, and the Coalition for Global Hearing Health to name a few. Many of these have local chapters and offer social gatherings. You can also get involved in organizations formed to help people around the world access technology or services for the D/deaf and hard of hearing.

 Check out hearingoutloud.net for resource links.

Social media is another way to make connections with people who have hearing loss. Virtually every social media platform has people talking about life with a hearing loss. Explore using keyword searches and hashtags.

FIND YOUR PEOPLE
JOURNAL ACTIVITY

Do you have people in your life who also have hearing loss? How do they support your well-being in a way which is different from other people in your life? If you don't know others with hearing loss, would you like to find them? What avenues might you pursue? Join an organization? Use a social media platform?

_____

_____

_____

_____

_____

_____

_____

_____

_____

_____

_____

_____

_____

_____

_____

_____

_____

_____

Conclusion of the Book

You have completed the final chapter in the *Becoming Hearing Empowered: A Guided Journal for the Deaf and Hard of Hearing.* I hope you have learned more about your hearing loss and more about yourself as a person with hearing loss. You decided to work through this journal as a way to learn more about living with hearing loss and to become "hearing empowered!"

Your time invested in this work has helped you:

- Learn how a growth mindset can open you to more possibilities in life. You don't have to stay stuck in the same circumstances you once were.
- Understand the basics of hearing loss science, the process of hearing, the anatomical structures affected that cause your hearing loss, and how to read an audiogram.
- Consider the ways your hearing loss impacts you emotionally.
- Apply strategies to propel you forward from the negative experiences you've endured.
- Think more deeply about how you identify yourself as a person with hearing loss.
- Diversify how you self-disclose and how you self-advocate.
- Develop new ways to improve communication with the important people in your life.
- Implement hearing loss specific self-care strategies to protect and replenish your energy.

FINAL THOUGHTS AND FEELINGS
JOURNAL ACTIVITY

What are your thoughts and feelings now having completed this journal? How do you hope it will improve your life? Are there portions of the book you'd like to revisit?

_____

_____

_____

_____

_____

_____

_____

_____

_____

_____

_____

_____

_____

_____

_____

_____

_____

_____

_____

_____

_____

Please reach out to me with any questions or suggestions on how this book can be more helpful or accurate at katherine@hearingoutloud.net.

Best wishes—

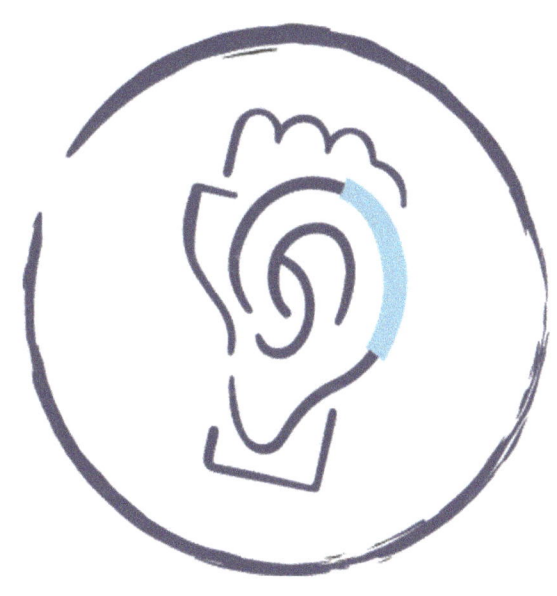

daily log

Date	Plan for today
Completed today	
Action plan	
Thoughts and gratitudes	
Affirmation	

Date	Plan for today
Completed today	
Action plan	
Thoughts and gratitudes	
Affirmation	

daily log

Date	Plan for today
Completed today	
Action plan	
Thoughts and gratitudes	
Affirmation	

Date	Plan for today
Completed today	
Action plan	
Thoughts and gratitudes	
Affirmation	

daily log

Date	Plan for today
Completed today	
Action plan	
Thoughts and gratitudes	
Affirmation	

Date	Plan for today
Completed today	
Action plan	
Thoughts and gratitudes	
Affirmation	

daily log

Date	Plan for today
Completed today	
Action plan	
Thoughts and gratitudes	
Affirmation	

Date	Plan for today
Completed today	
Action plan	
Thoughts and gratitudes	
Affirmation	

daily log

Date	Plan for today
Completed today	
Action plan	
Thoughts and gratitudes	
Affirmation	

Date	Plan for today
Completed today	
Action plan	
Thoughts and gratitudes	
Affirmation	

daily log

Date	Plan for today
Completed today	
Action plan	
Thoughts and gratitudes	
Affirmation	

Date	Plan for today
Completed today	
Action plan	
Thoughts and gratitudes	
Affirmation	

daily log

Date	Plan for today
Completed today	
Action plan	
Thoughts and gratitudes	
Affirmation	

Date	Plan for today
Completed today	
Action plan	
Thoughts and gratitudes	
Affirmation	

daily log

Date	Plan for today
Completed today	
Action plan	
Thoughts and gratitudes	
Affirmation	

Date	Plan for today
Completed today	
Action plan	
Thoughts and gratitudes	
Affirmation	

daily log

Date	Plan for today
Completed today	
Action plan	
Thoughts and gratitudes	
Affirmation	

Date	Plan for today
Completed today	
Action plan	
Thoughts and gratitudes	
Affirmation	

daily log

Date	Plan for today
Completed today	
Action plan	
Thoughts and gratitudes	
Affirmation	

Date	Plan for today
Completed today	
Action plan	
Thoughts and gratitudes	
Affirmation	

daily log

Date	Plan for today
Completed today	
Action plan	
Thoughts and gratitudes	
Affirmation	

Date	Plan for today
Completed today	
Action plan	
Thoughts and gratitudes	
Affirmation	

daily log

Date	Plan for today
Completed today	
Action plan	
Thoughts and gratitudes	
Affirmation	

Date	Plan for today
Completed today	
Action plan	
Thoughts and gratitudes	
Affirmation	

daily log

Date	Plan for today
Completed today	
Action plan	
Thoughts and gratitudes	
Affirmation	

Date	Plan for today
Completed today	
Action plan	
Thoughts and gratitudes	
Affirmation	

daily log

Date	Plan for today
Completed today	
Action plan	
Thoughts and gratitudes	
Affirmation	

Date	Plan for today
Completed today	
Action plan	
Thoughts and gratitudes	
Affirmation	

daily log

Date	Plan for today
Completed today	
Action plan	
Thoughts and gratitudes	
Affirmation	

Date	Plan for today
Completed today	
Action plan	
Thoughts and gratitudes	
Affirmation	

journal

journal

journal

journal

_____

_____

_____

_____

_____

_____

_____

_____

_____

_____

_____

_____

_____

_____

_____

_____

_____

_____

_____

_____

_____

journal

journal

journal

journal

_____
_____
_____
_____
_____
_____
_____
_____
_____
_____
_____
_____
_____
_____
_____
_____
_____
_____
_____
_____
_____

journal

journal

_____
_____
_____
_____
_____
_____
_____
_____
_____
_____
_____
_____
_____
_____
_____
_____
_____
_____
_____
_____

draw

draw

draw

draw

draw

draw

BECOMING HEARING EMPOWERED

draw

draw

draw

AFFIRMATIONS

The way that I hear is a natural part of my life.

I grow in strength with every forward step I take.

I am proud of myself for even daring to try.

I am confident in my decision to wear hearing devices

I am confident in my decision to not wear hearing devices.

I like myself better each day.

Hearing loss is common, and this means that I am not alone in my experiences.

I have a powerful positive mental attitude.

I can ask for what I need without feeling embarrassed.

Hearing loss/Deafness won't stop me.

I feel powerful and confident.

I can nurture my new growth mindset.

Hearing aids/Cochlear implants support my positive well-being.

I know that my potential is unlimited.

I am proud of myself and my identity.

My assertiveness enriches my relationships.

I am a strong and confident self-advocate.

I can confidently explain my experience as a person with hearing loss.

I feel comfortable with the decisions I make.

I will show up for myself today as my own best self-advocate.

I can change my thoughts with positive assumptions.

My hearing aids/cochlear implants are amazing devices that can help me access the sounds around me.

AFFIRMATIONS

My feelings of self-esteem are strong.

I celebrate my unique identity as a person with hearing loss.

I deserve to have accommodations that give me equal opportunity to excel in life.

My feelings of self-worth are strong.

I have high self-confidence.

I am a good and caring person and deserve to be treated with respect.

I am capable of achieving success in my life.

There are people who love me and will be there for me when I need them.

I am allowed to make mistakes and learn from them.

I am grateful for my body and the way that it processes my environment.

I love myself, even when my hearing loss makes me feel frustrated or uneasy.

I can accomplish my goals.

I can communicate effectively.

I deserve healthy communication.

I deserve to be happy.

I can state what I need with confidence.

I deserve to be healthy.

I deserve to have a partner/friends/loved ones who understand my hearing loss.

I deserve to have a social network.

Some days will be more challenging than others, and this is a natural fact that I can accept.

Some days will be hard, but tomorrow could be better.

I have the power to be who I want to be.

I give myself permission to be exactly as I am.

ACKNOWLEDGMENTS

Jodi Costa for your guidance, formatting, editing, and overall support in getting this book past the finish line and into the readers' hands.

Kaitlin Walsh of Lyon Road Art for the stunning cover art and the ear anatomy diagram.

Kenzie Rybak for your countless hours providing thoughtful and emotionally-intuitive manuscript editing and feedback. Your writing skills and your ability to recognize what will touch the hearts of others show up on virtually every page of this book.

Alex Walters, Kevin Walters, and Danielle Mitchell for being my sounding board on our walks or hangouts on the deck. Your interest and encouragement pushed me forward to chip away at this huge endeavor.

Christine Rybak for your problem-solving, feedback, and cheerleading, not just for this project but for the entirety of my life.

Nina Buchanan for living authentically when bluffing and hiding are options people choose every day. While not dealing specifically with hearing loss, watching you uncover your own path in an often narrow-minded, stigma-filled world touches my heart.

Carol Rybak for finding the bravery to tell me. Those words opened our world to a lifetime of love and the opportunity to build this beautiful family together. Every day I am grateful for your genuine conviction that I can be more than my own limiting beliefs.

To **David Rybak**, my father, who tucked away every handmade book I made since the day I could write, draw, staple, and rubber cement my index card pages into something that mattered. I wanted to be a writer, I just didn't know what that would look like. I think you've always known.

ABOUT THE AUTHOR

Katherine Rybak has been a hard of hearing person since birth and is the founder of Hearing Out Loud®. Hearing Out Loud's mission is to move people forward in their lives as strong self-advocates who celebrate their identity, embrace technology, and confidently implement strategies to make meaningful connections within their community.

Katherine is a newly retired Teacher for the d/Deaf and Hard of Hearing, has earned her master's degree in education and is a National Board Certified Teacher. Katherine and her wife Carol have 3 grown children and 2 grandchildren. They live in their dream house on a little corner of Madison, Wisconsin. Katherine enjoys exploring her creativity in her upstairs writing/sewing studio, a walk in the sunshine with any of her 3 daughters, and playing on the floor with her grandchildren.

www.ingramcontent.com/pod-product-compliance
Lightning Source LLC
Chambersburg PA
CBHW041136120626
46547CB00020B/3009